MW01232937

Homemade magick

LON MILO DUQUETTE

Homemade.
magick

THE MUSINGS & MISCHIEF
OF A DO-IT-YOURSELF MAGUS

Llewellyn Publications
Woodbury, Minnesota

FIRST EDITION
First Printing, 2014

Cover design by Ellen Lawson
Cover images: iStockphoto.com/19726828/ © adventtr, iStockphoto.com/5013957/ ©
        sbayram, Tarot images from Tarot of Ceremonial Magick, created by Lon
        Milo DuQuette and painted by Constance Jean DuQuette. Published by
        Thelesis Aura: http://www.thelesisaura.com. Used with permission. Family
        photo courtesy of Lon Milo DuQuette.
Editing by Andrea Neff
Interior art by Llewellyn Art Department pages 44, 47–48 and 117
Interior photo credits on page 203

Special thanks go to Hymenaeus Beta, Frater Superior of Ordo Templi Orientis, for his kind permission to print the various excerpts from the works of Aleister Crowley; and to North Atlantic books for permission to print material adapted from the translation by Blaise Daniel Staples of the *Homeric Hymn to Demeter*, originally published in *The Road to Eleusis: Unveiling the Secret of the Mysteries* by R. Gordon Wasson, Albert Hofmann, and Carl A. P. Ruck, Thirtieth Anniversary Edition published by North Atlantic Books, Copyright © 2008 by the R. Gordon Wasson Estate. Reprinted by permission of the publisher.

Llewellyn Publications is a registered trademark of Llewellyn Worldwide Ltd.

Library of Congress Cataloging-in-Publication Data
DuQuette, Lon Milo, 1948–
  Homemade magick : the musings & mischief of a do-it-yourself magus / by
Lon Milo DuQuette. — First Edition.
    pages cm
  Includes index.
  ISBN 978-0-7387-3298-5
  1. DuQuette, Lon Milo, 1948- 2. Magicians—United States—Biography.
3. Magic. I. Title.
  BF1598.D86A3 2014
  133.4'3—dc23

                     2014016198

Llewellyn Worldwide Ltd. does not participate in, endorse, or have any authority or responsibility concerning private business transactions between our authors and the public.
    All mail addressed to the author is forwarded, but the publisher cannot, unless specifically instructed by the author, give out an address or phone number.
    Any Internet references contained in this work are current at publication time, but the publisher cannot guarantee that a specific location will continue to be maintained. Please refer to the publisher's website for links to authors' websites and other sources.

Llewellyn Publications
A Division of Llewellyn Worldwide Ltd.
2143 Wooddale Drive
Woodbury, MN 55125-2989
www.llewellyn.com

Printed in the United States of America

Other Books by Lon Milo DuQuette

Ask Baba Lon: Candid Answers to Questions of Life and Magick
(New Falcon Publications, 2011)

Aleister Crowley: Revolt of the Magicians
(Orobas Press, 2011)

Low Magick
(Llewellyn Publications, 2010)

Dr. John Dee and Edward Kelley
(Weiser Books, 2008)

Accidental Christ: The Story of Jesus (as Told by His Uncle)
(Thelesis Aura, 2007)

Enochian Vision Magick: An Introduction and Practical Guide to the Magick of
The Key to Solomon's Key: Secrets of Magic and Masonry
(CCC Publishing, 2006)

The Book of Ordinary Oracles
(Weiser Books, 2005)

The Magick of Aleister Crowley: A Handbook of the Rituals of Thelema
(Weiser Books, 2003)

Understanding Aleister Crowley's Thoth Tarot: An Authoritative Examination
of the World's Most Fascinating and Magical Tarot Cards
(Weiser Books, 2003)

The Chicken Qabalah of Rabbi Lamed Ben Clifford: A Dilettante's Guide to
What You Do and Do Not Need to Know to Become a Qabalist
(Weiser Books, 2001)

My Life with the Spirits: The Adventures of a Modern Magician
(Weiser Books, 1999)

Angels, Demons & Gods of the New Millenium: Musings on Modern Magick
(Weiser Books, 1997)

Tarot of Ceremonial Magick: A Pictorial Synthesis of Three Great Pillars of
Magick (Astrology, Enochian Magick, Goetia)
(Weiser Books, 1995)

Aleister Crowley's Illustrated Goetia
(co-authored with Christopher S. Hyatt, PhD,
New Falcon Publications, 1992)

Taboo: Sex, Religion & Magick
(co-authored with Christopher S. Hyatt, PhD,
New Falcon Publications, 1992)
Enochian World of Aleister Crowley: Enochian Sex Magick
(co-authored with Christopher S. Hyatt, PhD,
New Falcon Publications, 1991)
Sex Magick, Tantra & Tarot: The Way of the Secret Lover
(co-authored with Christopher S. Hyatt, PhD,
New Falcon Publications, 1991)

Intent is the mechanics through which spirit
transforms itself into material reality.

DEEPAK CHOPRA[1]

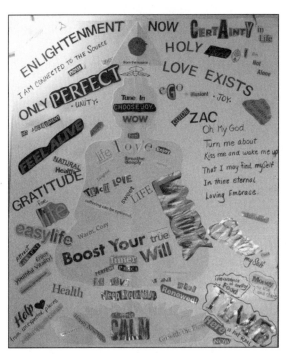

Constance's "dream board" placed squarely over the washing machine.

---

1. Deepak Chopra, *The Spontaneous Fulfillment of Desire: Harnessing the Infinite Power of Coincidence* (New York: Three Rivers Press, 2004), p. 115.

SPECIAL THANKS

This little book is dedicated to the talented, generous, supportive, and forgiving friends and brethren who have since 1975 taught Constance and me *everything*. All that is good and true, awesome and holy, has poured like liquid light from the cornucopia that is the love of these dear souls.

Most especially to our dear friends and fellow homemade magicians Doug and Karen James, and Steve and Judy Abbott, we say thank you. We are so lucky to have once again incarnated with you.

Special thanks also go to Hymenaeus Beta, Frater Superior of Ordo Templi Orientis, for his kind permission to print the various excerpts from the works of Aleister Crowley; and to North Atlantic books for permission to print material adapted from the translation by Blaise Daniel Staples of the *Homeric Hymn to Demeter*, originally published in *The Road to Eleusis: Unveiling the Secret of the Mysteries* by R. Gordon Wasson, Albert Hofmann, and Carl A. P. Ruck, Thirtieth Anniversary Edition published by North Atlantic Books, Copyright © 2008 by the R. Gordon Wasson Estate. Reprinted by permission of the publisher.

Contents

Nebraska Maids

It does not matter much whom we live with in this world,
but it matters a great deal whom we dream of.
WILLA CATHER (NEBRASKAN), "A GOLD SLIPPER"

Like my father and brother before me, I was born in Southern California and journeyed to rural Nebraska to find a bride. There is something primeval and mammalian about being born and raised in one part of the world, then traveling to some strange and exotic land to fall in love and find a mate. Indeed, many classic fairy tales tell of a wandering prince who wins his dream princess in a foreign land.

Obviously, I'm not a prince, and Nebraska isn't exactly strange or exotic; but for a seven-year-old boy (rudely uprooted from his home in sunny Southern California), the "Cornhusker State" in 1956 was a grotesque nightmare. I felt like a shell-shocked war refugee—cruelly banished from my beachfront homeland and exiled to a dusty, chigger-infested wilderness populated by coarse barbarians who didn't trim the fat off their ham sandwiches, considered Jell-O with a dollop of mayonnaise to be "salad," and for some strange reason called lunch "dinner."

I languished for a full decade in small-town Nebraska, fantasizing that I'd be rescued by a flying saucer and plotting my escape back to the hip and trendy land of my birth. At night I dreamed I smelled the beach; I actually tasted the salt of the ocean on my dream tongue. Throughout my decade of Nebraska exile, California grew in my imagination into a mythical Ithaca. But unlike the hero Odysseus, I had no queen waiting for me on the golden shores of my lost kingdom. For that illusive treasure I would need to grow up and find a *Nebraska woman*.

Perhaps it is because Nebraska breeds a very special woman—the kind of woman who stoically endures some of the most brutal winters on earth for months on end when bitter arctic winds blast down from Canada and sweep through the Dakotas foiled by nothing higher than prairie grass; the kind of woman who, when the mercury tops a humid 110 degrees, will wash her hair in the kitchen sink and blithely brush it dry on the back porch; the kind of woman who, without blinking an eye, will lance a boil, stanch a bleeding wound, or gut a fish; the kind of woman who will, with firm and loving hands, tenderly end the life of a suffering dog or cat.

Despite all the cruelties and hardships this land inflicts upon them, these remarkable women love Nebraska. If destiny conspires to pluck them up and carry them off to faraway places, their hearts remain rooted in the thick, black loam of the prairie. They pine for that terrible and beautiful place like lovesick maidens who never recover from an adolescent romance. The change of seasons pulls their hearts back to the awesome land that wooed them so roughly. Like the majestic sandhill cranes, their souls migrate year after year back to the cruel and fragrant Eden of the Platte River Valley—a world the Pawnees called the "happy hunting grounds."

DuQuette men must be a lot like Nebraska, for it takes a Nebraska woman to love us, to endure us, to inexplicably draw strength from our brash insensitivity and other unmanly DuQuette virtues a lesser woman might mistake for self-absorbed stupidity.

In 1966, my Nebraska odyssey ended. I returned to California immediately after high school graduation and began classes at Orange Coast College in Costa Mesa. College life in Southern California in 1966–67 was a very rich and colorful experience, little of which had anything to do with academics. The popularity of mind-expanding drugs and the social and political upheavals of the day (triggered by the Civil Rights movement and the war in Vietnam) were far more interesting to me than my English and drama classes. I was profoundly affected by my experiences with LSD and soon began to seriously turn my attention to the study and practice of Eastern mysticism, especially Hindu philosophy and yoga.

My brother, Marc, was my mystical fellow traveler on most of these psychedelic journeys. He would often volunteer to be my sane and sober babysitter and "guide" while I "tripped." I, on alternate occasions, would do the same for him. The experiences were spiritual journeys we took very seriously, and the deeper we plunged into the depths of our own psyches, the more we knew that self-realization was the most important thing a human being can achieve during his or her time on earth.

One afternoon, the day before a full moon, we decided to drive out to the desert and take a massive dose of LSD together. We watched the full moon set in the west and the sun rise in the east. We vowed we would not return from the desert "until we were holy men." I wrote about this event at greater length in an earlier autobiography,[2] so I won't bore you with the details here. I will, instead, jump to the quiet moments a few hours after that eternal day in the desert.

We managed to drive safely back to Costa Mesa late in the afternoon. We were still quite high but confident enough in our ability to "maintain" in public to visit our favorite tavern. It was there, sitting on the most comfortable barstool in the universe, my acid-soaked brain still soaring through the rarefied clouds of Technicolor consciousness, that I realized I would be incapable of safely controlling the awesome and terrible nuclear fusion of consciousness that was taking place in my cranium. I started to see the big picture. If I were to continue my incarnational adventure, I would need something, some*one*, to ground me, to anchor me, to hold my feet to the ground before I exploded spectacularly (but prematurely) on the launch pad of life.

I needed a *Nebraska woman.*

---

2. *My Life with the Spirits* (York Beach, ME: Weiser Books, 1999).

I had dated Constance on and off during our junior and senior years of high school in Nebraska, and when I returned to California we kept in touch by old-fashioned letters. We were friends. She liked my progressive politics. I liked her hair. We'd certainly never discussed marriage. But now I could not imagine a future without her. More accurately, I saw quite clearly that there wasn't a future without her. Perched high upon the oracular tripod of my psychedelic barstool, I saw the future set in stone, as fixed and immutable as the past.

I called her from the payphone near the pinball machine and proposed marriage. To this day I really can't tell you why I asked, and to this day she doesn't know why she said yes. But, like a traditional Hindu couple whose parents sealed the marriage contract when they were babies, we dutifully surrendered to our destinies then and there.

We've been married for forty-seven years. Neither one of us can tell you exactly why.

Do we love each other? Yes, of course we love each other. Are we happy? Well…sometimes yes, sometimes no. But at least we've grown wise enough to realize that ultimately one person can never make another person happy, and even if we could, love is bigger than happiness. Each individual in this world, whether married or single, is responsible for his or her own condition of happiness or unhappiness.

What does all this have to do with *homemade magick*? My answer is simple. The edifice of my life—my home, my work, my magick—is built upon a foundation that is the love, the support, the opposition, the criticism, the irritation, the wisdom, and the ruthless condemnation of this Nebraska maid. Constance is a supernatural force of nature—an awesome and terrible magical being, a goddess, a devil, an angel, a harpy, a demon. She is also the archetypal wife, mother, and grandmother, but greater than all these things she is her own unique universe. She is, in every relevant sense of the term, a living saint.[3]

Take it from me: it's not easy being the mortal husband of a saint. Any envy you might feel for me and my extraordinarily good matrimo-

---

3. In 1976, Hymenaeus Alpha (Grady McMurtry), head of Ordo Templi Orientis, dubbed Constance "Saint Constance of the Well."

nial fortune must be tempered by an outpouring of pity, for even though I am blessed with many unique and admirable qualities, I am *not* a saint. It's important that you remain mindful of this cruel irony as I attempt to relate a few of our family adventures in the pages of this book.

Constance and I took no vows to each other during our homemade wedding ceremony of so long ago. We promised each other nothing. Nonetheless, for over forty-seven years, for better or worse, in sickness and in health, this Nebraska maid has been and remains the *home* in my *homemade magick*.

PART I

Initiation

Rant of the Homemade Magician

Doing magick is not what magick is about.
The goal in magick is to be a magician.

I'm not altogether happy with the title I've chosen for this book. It's a bit misleading, because ultimately all magick is an intensely personal endeavor—by definition *homemade*. Of course, a person can be formally trained (or at least educated) in one or more of the classic magical systems, such as qabalistic, Wiccan, Druidic, Native American, Solomonic, Enochian, etc., or one can be part of a highly structured and formally structured magical group or mystery school, such as a coven or a lodge of esoteric Masons, the Golden Dawn, Servants of the Light, or Ordo Templi Orientis (O.T.O.). One might even be lucky enough to be privately tutored by an experienced and illuminated magical adept. But as magicians—indeed, as human beings—we have only one universe *in which* to work, and only one universe *with which* to work. That universe is ourselves.

3

No matter what your circumstances may be, when it comes time to perform real magick, your magick can only be executed by, for, and through the agency of *you alone*. The most I can hope to accomplish in writing a book of this nature is to share a few scattered accounts of my own life and magical career and encourage you to consider how my experiences might best be translated and applied to the unique circumstances of your own life. To that end, I think it would be helpful if I started by giving you a quick review of my background and current magical milieu.

I was born on July 11, 1948, in Long Beach, California.[4] I moved with my parents and older brother to Columbus, Nebraska, in 1956 and returned to Southern California after high school graduation in 1966. I became a professional musician at the age of fourteen and made my living as a songwriter and recording artist through my mid-twenties.

I have been married to Constance since 1967. We have one son, Jean-Paul, who is a university professor in Japan. I speak English and only the tiniest fragments of French and Spanish. This means that my entire education, magical and otherwise, has been acquired from texts written in or translated into the English language. I quit college (I was pretending to be a drama major) after only one year and studied acting for a short time at the Lee Strasberg Theatre and Film Institute in Hollywood. I hold no academic degrees.

A series of psychedelically triggered mystical experiences in 1966 through 1971 led me to seek preliminary yoga instruction, and I also dabbled in various meditation techniques and practices of Eastern mysticism at Paramahansa Yogananda's Self-Realization Fellowship and the Vedanta Society. From 1971 to 1975, I studied (via correspondence-course instruction) aspects of the Western mystery traditions, through the Rosicrucian

---

4. I am sixty-five years old at the time of this writing.

Order (AMORC),[5] the Builders of the Adytum (B.O.T.A),[6] and the Traditional Martinist Order (TMO).[7]

Around this time, I became passionately interested in the written works of Aleister Crowley. In 1975 I met Grady Louis McMurtry (aka Hymenaeus Alpha, 777) and his then wife, Phyllis Seckler McMurtry (aka Soror Meral), who initiated me into two of Crowley's magical organizations, Ordo Templi Orientis (O.T.O.) and A∴A∴ Before Crowley's death in 1947, the McMurtrys had both been disciples of Crowley. Grady had received O.T.O.'s highest initiatory degree directly from Crowley in England, and Phyllis had been the personal student of Crowley's acolyte Jane Wolfe. The McMurtrys, in turn, introduced me to Francis (Israel) Regardie, former secretary to Crowley and a celebrated occult author in his own right.

In 1976 I was passed into the next degree in O.T.O. in Dublin, California. Assisting the McMurtrys with this ceremony was Helen Parsons-Smith, another Crowley contemporary and the widow of both Wilfred T. Smith (former O.T.O. North American Grand Master) and John Whiteside (Jack) Parsons. Parsons had been an eminent rocket scientist, a developer of jet-powered take-off and solid rocket fuel. He was one of the founding members of Jet Propulsion Laboratory, the forerunner of NASA. This brilliant magician/scientist was posthumously honored by the space agency for his contributions to the program by having a crater on the Moon named for him.

In 1978 I was authorized by Grady McMurtry to establish and operate a lodge of O.T.O. in Southern California, and I remain its Lodge Master to this day. In 1996 I was appointed U.S. National Deputy Grand Master of O.T.O. by McMurtry's successor, Hymenaeus Beta.

---

5. The Ancient and Mystical Order Rosae Crucis (AMORC) is an international philosophical and humanistic fraternal organization. At the time of my active membership, it was headquartered in San Jose, California.

6. Builders of the Adytum (B.O.T.A.) is a nonprofit religious organization based in Los Angeles that was founded by Paul Foster Case (1884–1954).

7. At the time of my membership in TMO, it was closely affiliated with the AMORC organization.

In January of 1978, the DuQuette family played host to the head of the O.T.O.—Caliph Hymenaeus Alpha, 777, IX° (Grady L. McMurtry)—at our home in Costa Mesa, California. This picture was snapped just prior to Grady signing our lodge charter and officiating at our first round of initiations. We have always run the lodge out of our home, and remain the oldest continually operating O.T.O. lodge in the world.

I first met McMurtry on November 14, 1975, just one day before he initiated me into the Minerval Degree (0°) of O.T.O. in the garage temple of his home (and the home of his then wife, Phyllis Seckler McMurtry) in Dublin, California. Constance was initiated Minerval in the backyard of the same Dublin residence a few months later.

Twelve years after this picture was taken, Constance and I had the pleasure of initiating our son, Jean-Paul (pictured here at the age of five), on the occasion of his eighteenth birthday in the backyard of our home in Costa Mesa.

Throughout the years I have supported myself and my family in a number of ways. I was a singer-songwriter and recording artist[8] in the late 1960s and early 1970s and afterward held a string of low-paying positions in manufacturing, property management, and advertising, all of which allowed me quite a bit of flexibility to pursue my personal magical studies and practices.

In 1988 Constance and I initiated Dr. Christopher S. Hyatt into our O.T.O. lodge, and over the next few years he and I collaborated on a number of writing projects that opened up an exciting new chapter in my magical and professional life.

So there you have it. In the last forty years, my homemade magical career has included a lot of work with various spiritual disciplines and systems, instructors, and magical orders. I will be the first to admit that I have been very lucky, and my experiences are most likely very different from your own. But you would be gravely mistaken if you believed that because my life and background are in some ways different from yours, it means you are somehow at a disadvantage in your work as a magician.

Like it or not, the cards you've been dealt in life make up exactly the hand you need to play. To be a magician, you do *not* need to be the personal student of an adept, and you do *not* need to belong to any magical order or society. You are and always will be your own universe. You are a homemade magick school with one teacher and one student. You are an entire mystic order of one. And even if someday you happen to come under the tutelage of some great master, even if you join and become an adept of a powerful occult order, you will still be facing exactly the same obstacles and challenges you are facing right now; you will still be required to do all the magick yourself; you will remain forever a solitary practitioner.

This is not to say that all of us are not influenced and affected by others, or that our actions, thoughts, and behavior don't affect our environment. If other people are healed or gain a level of enlightenment as a

---

8. I wrote and recorded with my partner, Charles Dennis Harris. We called our band *Charley D. & Milo* and recorded and released two singles and an album on the Epic Records label and wrote songs for and recorded with other recording artists, most notably Johnny Rivers.

byproduct of *your* self-realization and self-transformation, that's great. But ultimately you are a solo act; and your temple, your workshop, your laboratory, and your universe are your own body, your own brain, your own soul.

Doing magick is not what magick is about. *The goal in magick is to be a magician.* The only thing the magician can actually change with magick is the *magician.* This book is intended to be helpful and instructive, but you'll be neither helped nor instructed if you think you can accomplish the Great Work by blindly replicating magical operations exactly as described by me or anyone else. That's not how it works.

Magick is a process—a step-by-step journey of self-directed, self-willed personal evolution. That process must take place within the context of whatever opportunities, liabilities, assets, obstacles, restrictions, and fortunes (good or ill) your life circumstances have given you and those that you make for yourself.

You might be single or married, or your relationship status might be complicated. You might have children. You might have a corporate or professional job, or you might be an artist or a musician. You might be employed, unemployed, or retired. You might be independently wealthy or a penniless ascetic. You might be socially and politically conservative or liberal. Your circumstances might even be such that you have to keep your magical interests a secret from everyone around you, or you might be able to burst madly out of the wizard's closet in public.

Whatever your situation, once you realize you are a magician, it will be impossible for you to remove the magick from any aspect of your existence. What you do for a living will no longer be just a job, it will be a magick job. Your relationships will be with magical beings. Your hobbies will be magick, and your love life will be magick. Your likes, dislikes, fears, dreams, ambitions, and even shortcomings and vices will be magick. It's all magick because you never stop being a magician.

The DuQuette magical family unit, Costa Mesa, California, c. 1975: Lon (Papa), Constance (Mama), Jean-Paul (our "Little Buddha"), and Shep (dog).

———

In this book, I will share a few examples of how I've made the magical arts an integral facet of my life. But in addition to that (and even more importantly), I will try to offer you a few glimpses of how a magician interprets each and every seemingly mundane and *un*-magical event of everyday life as the *magical adventure* it truly is. I hope that you will be able to somehow apply my examples to the unique circumstances of your own life.

Your homemade magical adventure begins when you first *wake up* to the fact that you are quite literally *asleep*. We will all wake up eventually, but what differentiates magicians from our sleepy neighbors is that we are ready and willing to jump-start the waking-up process. Formally and with full intent, we stir from our slumbering stupor and declare to the gods, "I am waking up now! Let my journey begin!"

Who Are You?

The Caterpillar and Alice looked at each other for some time in silence: at last the Caterpillar took the hookah out of its mouth, and addressed her in a languid, sleepy voice.

"Who are YOU?" said the Caterpillar.

This was not an encouraging opening for a conversation. Alice replied, rather shyly, "I—I hardly know, sir, just at present—at least I know who I WAS when I got up this morning, but I think I must have been changed several times since then."

LEWIS CARROLL, *ALICE'S ADVENTURES IN WONDERLAND*, CH. 5

Every journey has a *destination*, every journey has a *path* or paths to that destination, and every journey has *obstacles* and challenges along the way.

For magicians, our destination is supreme enlightenment (union and absolute integration) with the Supreme Intelligence of the cosmos—complete identity with the universal consciousness.

The path is (at least for a little while) the magical arts and disciplines.

The obstacles and challenges on the path are all our shortcomings, character flaws, vices, bad habits, fears, imbalances, misperceptions, and personal demons that are currently distracting us and preventing us from waking up from the dreamworld of un-enlightenment.

Before we can even discuss the destination or the path or the obstacles, however, we need to identify just who it is that will be taking this journey. We need a traveler, a sojourner, a hero, someone to experience the trip. The journey needs *you*. It sounds simple enough, but it really isn't. Who you are (or who you think you are) is vitally important. Allow me to digress for a moment.

Constance and I were very young when we first started living together. She was nineteen years old and I was eighteen. (Yes, she's almost six months older than I.) From the very beginning of our relationship, we identified ourselves as spiritual adventurers, cosmic gypsies, who had once again incarnated to pick up where we left off ... to continue our quest and take the next step toward enlightenment. Admittedly, we were romantic and naive. But we were also spiritually audacious, and we delighted in our explorations of what were for us exotic foreign religions and cultures. We enjoyed fantasizing about our previous incarnations. We playfully identified ourselves as our own homemade mythological characters on a timeless quest. We assumed whimsical Native American names (Sleeping Bear and Smiling Squirrel—guess which one I was) and speculated about medieval lives as court jester and scullery maid, or Mandarin lord and youngest wife.

We hand-painted bizarre (and patently offensive) anti-Christmas cards and mailed them to our clueless and easily shocked relatives, and whenever possible we wore our new and colorful mystical opinions and personas on our sleeves.

As sophomoric and silly as these fanciful lovers' games were, they taught us how to begin discovering who we are. They served to seriously establish and formulate our magical identities and train our imaginations.

Constance and I were fortunate that our youth and silliness allowed us to fall quite naturally into the spirit of the game of magical self-identification. For others, it might take a little more effort. No matter what your age, background, or circumstances, the process must begin by asking yourself, "Who am I?"

So ... who are you?

Don't answer with your name, because you know darn well that's not who you are. Don't try to avoid this question, because it's a big one. Unless you can come up with some kind of answer to this question, there won't be a *magician* to work the magick.

Well, who *are* you?

Traditionally, the phrase "Know thyself" was chiseled in stone above the threshold of the temples of the ancient mysteries. That sounds like wise and serious advice, doesn't it? But think about it: the chances of you truly knowing yourself anytime soon are slim to none!

Know thyself? Give me a break! Even though those words represent the *first* piece of advice you get at the beginning of your magical career, the cold hard fact remains that true self-realization is likely to be the very *last thing* that's ever going to happen to you. Who and what you *really are* will be the final revelation in life's great mystery play— the last tiny bit of information your (by then) near-infinitely expanded consciousness will process in the blinding micro-seconds just before you ecstatically sizzle into pure undifferentiated Godhead—

Oh! *THAT'S* what I am! *Phssssssssssssssss.*!

But if you don't know who or what you are, there obviously can't be a *you* to take the journey. There is no *you* to choose the destination, no *you* to find the path, no *you* to overcome the obstacles, no *you* for the magical universe to torture and delight and broaden and purify and perfect, no hook of a *you* upon which to hang the great adventure of your destiny.

But don't worry. There *is* a real *you* in there somewhere, and even though you currently don't have a clue about who or what you are, the discovery process has to begin somewhere! You begin by first *pretending you know who you are.*

Yes, like everything else in life, you are going to have to *fake it till you make it!* There's no other way to start. Sound silly? Sound irrational? Sound insane? Sound like cheating? Welcome to the world of homemade magick! No need to wait for a guru, or a magical mentor, or some lofty adept, or a high priest or priestess, or some mysterious secret-society hierophant to initiate you. You just have to haul off and do it yourself.

Go ahead! Roll up the sleeves on your magical robe and start faking it till you make it. Start right now by *pretending* you know who you are! It's easy. You begin by renaming yourself, by giving yourself a new homemade identity—a *magical motto*.

TWO

Your Homemade Magical Motto

Halt! Who goes there?

There's no time like the present. (That's more than a cliché, it's a cosmological fact!) It's time to give yourself a magical motto. But before you go changing things, I want you to first take a moment to appreciate the magick of your given name, because in actuality it is your first and most powerful magical motto.

I'm lucky. I like my name. Right up until the time my father died, he insisted that I never change or even alter the spelling of my name. As a child I complained to him about "Lon Milo" being so weird and different. "You have a *magic* name," he insisted. "Don't ever change it. Don't even change the spelling or capitalization." Dad certainly wasn't a qabalist or mystic, so I'm not sure how he was defining the word *magic*, but he was very serious and insistent.

Your given name *is* profoundly magical. Your name is the magical incantation that evokes you! Think about it. The sound of your own name brings you alive to the awareness of yourself. When you are in a public place or a room full of people and you hear your name being called, what happens in your mind?

"Here I am," you say in your soul. You remember *you are you!* You identify yourself *to* yourself. You acknowledge your presence, your life, your existence. The sound of your own name *wakes you up*, and that's precisely what a magical motto should do.

If you already have a magical motto, you might consider coming up with a new one. Go ahead. Don't be shy. Think about renaming yourself. Make it something that sounds cool and perhaps even a little pretentious. The best magical motto is a word or phrase that represents your current understanding of the universe and reality, or expresses the loftiest goals and aspirations you have right at *this moment* in your spiritual evolution. As time passes and you grow wiser and more insightful, you will most likely want to trade in the old motto and choose a new and improved one—one that more accurately reflects your increased level of enlightenment (not to mention your expanding capacity for pretense).

So, are you ready to start pretending you know who you are?

Then get serious (or very silly) for a moment and think of the absolute highest spiritual concept or aspiration you can dream up. It doesn't have to be short. Go ahead and name yourself Frater "All the Power in the Universe Is Inside My Head" (A.T.P.I.T.U.I.I.M.H.), or Soror "The Archangels Grovel and Bow Down to My Awesome Coolness" (T.A.G.A.B.D.T.M.A.C.), or Frater "I Don't Care What You Think About My Tie I'm Going to Wear It" (I.D.C.W.Y.T.A.M.T.I.G.T.W.I.).

You'll probably want to choose something less silly than these examples, but don't worry about it sounding too audacious, corny, or pretentious, because chances are, *anything* you think of right now will be profoundly inadequate. For the time being, however, you just have to be *temporarily comfortable* with identifying yourself with that word or statement. Just pick a motto and stick with it until you outgrow it.

I can always tell when Constance has changed her motto. A new little sign appears suddenly in the kitchen on the *altar* of our refrigerator door. Her first motto was *Beauty, Growth, Balance.* A few years later she became Sister *So What!* For years after that she simply identified with the prime number *83* because of something she read in an Aleister Crowley essay on numbers, where he wrote: "83: Consecration: love in its highest form: energy, freedom, amrita, aspiration. The root of the idea of romance plus religion."[9]

Our refrigerator altar. Most everyone decorates the refrigerator door. Constance's choice of objects includes her past and present magical mottos and sacred images and aphorisms.

———

Fruitless Love and Aimless Toil was the next motto to appear on the refrigerator door, followed a couple years later by the disturbingly profound (and oddly capitalized) statement *iAM FINISHED.* Presently she is *Glory to God.*

My first attempt at a magical motto wasn't a motto at all but a number. My father's admonition to never change my name got me thinking

---

9. Aleister Crowley, *777 and Other Qabalistic Writings of Aleister Crowley: Including Gematria and Sepher Sephiroth* (York Beach, ME: Weiser Books, 1986), p. xxv.

about the qabalistic virtues inherent in the letters of my own name. I converted the letters into their Hebrew equivalents using a chart I created similar to this:

A	1	N	50
B	2	O	70, 6
C	8, 20, 300	P	80
D	4	Q	100
E	5	R	200
F	6	Sh, S	300, 60
G	3	Th, T, Tz	400, 9, 90
H	5	U	6
I	10	V	6
J	10	W	6
K	20	X	90
L	30	Y	10
M	40	Z	90

L = ל = 30
O = ע = 70
N = נ = 50

M = מ = 40
I = י = 10
L = ל = 30
O = ע = 70

D = ד = 4
U = ו = 6
Q = ק = 100
U = ו = 6
E = ה = 5
T = ט = 9
T = ט = 9
E = ה = 5
<u>   </u>
444

There are other ways to use Hebrew letters to spell out "Lon Milo DuQuette," but to me, this was the simplest and most straightforward rendering of the name. I was absolutely thrilled that my magick name added up to such a cool-looking number. (It was like a poor man's 666!) I consulted a table of important qabalistic words and their number equivalents and, to my disappointment, discovered that 444 was not a number to get too excited about. Multiples of 111 are always nice, and there are many ways to play with 444 that generate material to meditate on, but the most important thing I got out of the whole exercise was a certain sense of identity and the simple realization that it was "my" number and one of the reasons my name (and my life) was magical. It is the reason that I've always used my full name on anything and everything I publish. It is my stage name when I perform and my artist name when I record.

I chose my first formal magical motto in 1976 on the occasion of my reception as an A∴A∴ Probationer under the mentorship of Phyllis Seckler McMurtry. I chose for my motto a phrase that incorporated the initials of my name, L.M.D. I chose the three words "Liberty. Mastery. Dignity." To further abet my magical pretensions, I thought it would be extra elegant if I said it in French: *Liberté. Maîtrise. Dignité.* LMD is also the full spelling of the Hebrew letter Lamed ל,[10] which is traditionally assigned to the Tarot trump *Justice*. I felt my life could use the balance and discrimination that card represents.

One year later, when it came time for me to advance to the grade of Neophyte, I had grown more thoughtful (and a little less pompous). The ordeals and challenges of my probationary year had humbled me a bit, and my quest had become seriously personal and almost painfully simple. In what was becoming for me an increasingly complex universe, I realized that my only refuge, my only defense and protection, my only

---

10. Throughout my magical career, "L.M.D." has continued to serve me well. When I was consecrated Archbishop in the Ecclesia Gnostica Catholica (Gnostic Catholic Church), I took the ecclesiastical name "T Lamed." Also, I took the name Rabbi Lamed Ben Clifford (Lamed, Son of Clifford—Clifford was my father's name) as my *nom de plume* for my book *The Chicken Qabalah of Rabbi Lamed Ben Clifford* (York Beach, ME: Weiser Books, 2001).

hope for survival, my only hope for eventual self-mastery, rested on my ability to make and keep my spiritual aspirations as innocent and pure as possible. I chose the motto "Purity of Aspiration." Again, I rendered the phrase in French: *Pureté de l'aspiration.*

My subsequent mottos were *Hoathe IAIADA,* "True Worshipper of the Highest" in the Enochian Angelic language. Perhaps my favorite motto, and one that I thought might last me for the duration of this incarnation, was *Adeo Sat Bene,* Latin for "So far so good." Two years ago I accepted a new motto, "Only Love Is." Nostalgically I returned to French, *Seul l'amour est.*

Before we go any further, I would like you to pause now and settle the matter of *your* magical motto. If you already have a motto, fine. If you don't, I want you to create one right now. I'll wait…

Got it? Good!

Now, I want you to use your new motto to formally give birth to yourself as a homemade magician. I'm serious. Do you think you can become a magician just by reading about it? No. You actually have to *do stuff* yourself, stuff that nobody else can do for you. Sorry. This is your show. In order to give birth to yourself, you need to be your own mother, father, midwife, and baby. So please, listen up!

To illustrate their condition of spiritual blindness, candidates for initiation are (or at least have been since time immemorial) first blindfolded (hoodwinked) and bound hand and foot at the beginning of the ceremony. This is obviously a disturbing and uncomfortable position to find oneself in, and that's exactly why it's done. It's supposed to be disturbing and uncomfortable.

Before initiation, we dwell in the darkness, blind to the light of the greater reality that is enjoyed by the more spiritually enlightened. The candidate is unable to move forward effectively in this blind and ignorant state, unable to help himself or herself (let alone others) while in this sorry condition. As the ceremony proceeds, the bound and hoodwinked candidate "travels" (is led around) the temple or lodge room and is "taught" certain lessons. Eventually, as the candidate grows in knowledge and wisdom, the fetters are gradually removed. The climax of this part of the initiation ceremony is when the hoodwink is removed and the candidate is "brought to Light." But before this supreme moment, the candidate must first take an *oath*.

It is a scary thing being obliged to take a solemn oath in a ceremony like this. After all, you are making some very serious promises to people you can't even see while being tied up and completely at their mercy. In a temple or lodge room ceremony, the candidate must do a little soul-searching. Pragmatically, it is clear that unless he or she goes ahead and takes the oath, the initiation will not continue. The blindfold will stay on, and he or she will be removed from the initiation chamber and sent back into the outer darkness. Almost always the candidate dutifully proceeds to repeat the oath (no matter how it is worded), because in truth he or she is mildly confident that nothing too bad will happen.

Unless you've read ahead in this book, you're not sure exactly what you're going to promise in the oath you're about to take. But hey! Don't you trust me? (I hope you said no.) Come on! Even though you think it's silly, take the first step in your homemade initiation. It's disarmingly easy, and it will only take an eternal moment.

Start by taking a deep breath and pretending you are in the presence of the Supreme Intelligence of the universe (because you really *are*). Now recite the oath out loud with full magical intent. Then, if you don't see anything in the oath that you object to, *sign it* (right here in this book) using your new magical motto. If you don't like this oath, cross it out and make up another homemade oath, then recite it and sign it.

———

OATH

I, [Your magical motto],
in the presence of all I hold sacred, do hereby accept
absolute responsibility for my own condition of darkness and ignorance
and solemnly acknowledge and declare that ultimately
only I can bring myself to Light.

———

There! Wasn't that easy? It has only taken you countless incarnations (plus the number of years, days, hours, and seconds of this current lifetime) to get to this moment. Congratulations! The hardest part is over!

You are off to a good start and are now properly pretending to know who you are. You are now ready to undergo the ordeal of *initiation*.

Where do you go to be initiated?

How about initiating yourself—right at home!

THREE

Homemade Initiation

In all systems of religion is to be found a system of Initiation,
which may be defined as the process by which a man
comes to learn that unknown Crown.
ALEISTER CROWLEY, *LIBER LXI VEL CAUSAE* [11]

I didn't know what exactly to expect when I mailed my membership application and money to the Rosicrucian Order (AMORC) back in 1971,
but I was giddy at the thought of becoming a member of an honest-to-
goodness occult society of students and adepts. My brother, Marc, had
joined the organization (which advertised in magazines such as *Fate* and
Popular Mechanics) a number of months earlier and had shared a few of
his experiences. I knew I was signing up for a correspondence course—
an ongoing series of monographs that taught ancient occult principles
and exercises. I knew I was to faithfully study these monographs every
Thursday evening in the privacy of my home "temple." I also knew that

---

11. Aleister Crowley, *The Holy Books of Thelema, Liber LXI vel Causae* (York Beach,
ME: Samuel Weiser, 1983), p. xxxvii.

my study sessions would involve a certain amount of ceremony: a little candle lighting, incense burning, chanting, and meditation—just the kind of spooky stuff a wide-eyed, twenty-four-year-old fledgling mystic like Lon Milo DuQuette was looking for!

My first monograph arrived unceremoniously in the mail on a Thursday, a cosmic synchronicity I could only interpret as a direct message from the gods. I nervously waited for the sun to go down so I could open the envelope and let the magick begin. After dinner, I showered and dressed in my karate gi (the closest thing I had to magical vestments). Constance, who was pregnant with our soon-to-arrive and as-yet-unnamed baby, agreed to busy herself in the kitchen and living room while I sequestered myself in the bedroom with my candles, my incense, and my first mystical monograph. I opened the envelope, smelled the contents (yes, I smelled the contents), read the few introductory words, and realized I was to undergo right then and there a ceremony of *initiation*.

When I was a youngster in junior high school, the word *initiation* was a word to be feared. Initiation meant institutionalized bullying and torment inflicted by older students upon naive and fearful underclassmen. A Midwestern junior-high-school initiation meant getting your pants pulled off and hoisted up the flagpole, or discovering (too late) that someone had sprinkled itching powder in your jock.

Of course there are other, more innocuous kinds of initiation in life, but at the very least the word implied a preliminary fee or penalty one must pay before presuming to be part of an organization.

Initiate as a verb means "to begin." Initiation is simply a commencement. A *magical initiation* marks the beginning of a change—a mutation—an evolutionary step in the life of the magician who, if all goes well, will exit the initiatory chamber a different person from the one who blindly entered. Spiritual evolution is a series of these commencements. The magician formally recognizes the beginning of each new phase as he or she grows, step by step, degree by degree, in wisdom and understanding.

Formal initiatory societies were very popular in ancient Egypt, Greece, and various other Mediterranean and Asian cultures. The rites of initiation offered a more intelligent, elite, and esoteric spiritual experience than could be offered by the more crude and superstitious religions of the masses. Arguably, the most successful of the ancient initiatory societies was centered in the Greek city of Eleusis. The Eleusinian mysteries celebrated the agricultural mysteries of the goddess Demeter and her daughter Persephone for the better part of two thousand years.

The Eleusinian mysteries themselves had developed from the far older Mycenaean agricultural cults and the Egyptian rites of Isis and Osiris. The archetypal text that set the standard and formula for many of the initiatory societies was the *Egyptian Book of the Dead*, a magical text that on the surface presumes to counsel the recently deceased on how to navigate the obstacles and challenges of the afterlife in the timeless moments of the death coma. In doing so, the *Book of the Dead* also reveals the magical formula for the graduated process of self-induced consciousness expansion—the formula of initiation by degree.

Speculation about what actually went on during the ancient initiation ceremonies fills the pages of many occult books (some good, some laughably bad). Oddly enough, the process of speculation in and of itself is a vicarious initiatory experience, for in order to even contemplate the dynamics of an initiation, one has to put oneself in the place of both the candidate and the initiator.

To its credit, AMORC's little correspondence-course ceremonies of self-initiation were artfully crafted and presented in such a way that if the candidate was sincere and open to the moment, a degree of true initiation could take place. I can't speak for anyone else, but I can tell you without evasion, equivocation, or reservation that on that Thursday evening in 1971, I was profoundly *sincere and open to the moment*.

I allowed the printed words on the pages of that monograph to transport me to my own inner temple of initiation. There I met my magical self for the first time. There I pledged with every fiber of my being to discover the powers of my own soul and to use those powers to attain enlightenment and spiritual liberation for the benefit of myself and every monad of existence. I was ready for that moment. All I needed was a little shove—a little help and encouragement from those few words. The monograph may have given me the shove, but the initiation itself was entirely my own—a homemade initiation.

In the forty some years since that quiet evening, I've been the candidate in many initiation ceremonies. Some of them have required the dramatic and magical talents of many officers and have taken place in historic and richly adorned temples of gold and marble. Others have taken place in modest lodge rooms with only a handful of officers. Some have taken place under the stars or in converted garages and residential living rooms. In several of my initiations, the presiding officer was visibly intoxicated and the assisting officers ineptly read their lines from scripts they were seeing for the first time. No matter what the circumstances, I considered the experiences true initiations.

You're probably wondering, how on earth can someone consider a ceremony conducted by a drunken "master" assisted by untrained and incompetent officers to be a true and spiritual initiation?

My answer is simple. It is because all true initiations are *self-initiations*. No matter how simple or elaborate the ceremony, and no matter how skilled or competent the officers, the initiation itself takes place in the temple of your own soul. Your "application" is your *sincerity*, and your "initiation fee" is your desire and ability to be *open to the moment*.

My little AMORC monograph initiation was a real initiation. It couldn't have been more real, more effective, or more magical if I had been lying in the sarcophagus of the King's Chamber in the Great Pyramid of Giza and the presiding officers had been Lao Tzu, Buddha, Pythagoras, S. L. MacGregor Mathers, Aleister Crowley, Mark Twain, and the Dalai Lama.

All the initiation ceremonies I have subsequently passed through in my life have simply been amendments, "booster shots" to that first homemade initiation in my bedroom temple on that Thursday night so long ago.

So how about you? Are you feeling sincere and open to the moment? Have you reached a season in your life when all you need is a little shove to push you into the deep end of the pool of homemade magick? If your answer is yes, then you have just applied to and been accepted by the hidden hierophants of the Ancient and Mystical Order of Homemade Magicians (A.A.M.O.O.H.M.).

You may now open your initiation monograph.

FOUR

Homemade Ritual of Self-Initiation

I am that which remains.

The little ritual you are about to experience is a simple visualization accompanied by questions and answers (which you will have to ask and answer yourself). Ideally, you will have it memorized some day so you can do it lying down with your eyes closed. If you have access to simple recording equipment, you could even record the entire text and listen to it as you go through the visualizations. But right now, you need only find a quiet, comfortable place where you won't be disturbed for about fifteen minutes—a comfortable chair or even your bed can be your temple.

You may *purify* yourself by taking a bath or shower and then *consecrate* yourself by dabbing a little sweet-smelling oil on your forehead. You may, if you wish, dress yourself in a ceremonial robe. At the very least, you should wear clean and comfortable clothing. Then *purify* and *consecrate* your temple space by sprinkling a few drops of clean water in the quarters surrounding your chair or bed and then lighting a candle and perhaps a little incense.[12]

Once you are comfortably seated, imagine yourself standing in the sand outside of the Great Pyramid at Giza.

Sound corny? Never mind that. This is in your imagination, so you may as well have fun with it.

You have been summoned to appear for initiation at the Great Pyramid, but you see no way to enter. You don't know how you are to get in.

You hear a voice in the center of your brain.

Voice: **Knock upon the door of your heart.**

Think for a moment about what those words mean. Then gently pound your chest three times with one or both of your hands.

You instantly find yourself transported to the interior of the pyramid, to the room known as the King's Chamber. It is dimly lit, but you cannot see the source of the light. You are alone. Your attention is focused on the stone sarcophagus in the center of the chamber. You intuitively realize that the sarcophagus is for you. You instantly find yourself lying on your back in the stone-cool darkness of the sarcophagus.

Please take a moment to replay and experience this scene clearly in your imagination. If you'd like, rehearse it in your mind several times before continuing with the ceremony.

And now, a voice speaks to you from within the center of your head.

Voice: **Who are you?**

You answer with your new magical motto.

Voice: **Visualize the toes of your right foot.**

Focus your attention on the toes of your right foot and visualize them clearly.

Voice: **Are you the toes of your right foot?**

---

12. The protocols of ceremonial magick suggest that both the magician and the temple be purified with water and then consecrated with fire.

You think this is pretty silly question. Of course you are not the toes of your right foot, and you tell the voice that.

You: No, I am not.

Voice: Visualize the toes of your right foot disappearing.

You visualize the toes of your right foot painlessly dissolving away.

Voice: If those toes were missing, would you still be you?

Another silly question. Of course you would still be you if you were missing a few toes.

You: Yes. I am that which remains.

Voice: Now visualize the toes of your left foot.

You now focus your attention on the toes of your left foot and visualize them clearly.

Voice: Are you the toes of your left foot?

You: No, I am not.

Voice: Visualize the toes of your left foot disappearing.

Again, you visualize the toes of your left foot painlessly dissolving away.

Voice: If those toes were missing, would you still be you?

You: Yes. I am that which remains.

Voice: Now visualize your right foot.

Again you do so.

Voice: Are you your right foot?

You: No, I am not.

Voice: Visualize your right foot disappearing.

You do so again and throughout all the following questions.

Voice: If you had no right foot, would you still be you?

You: Yes. I am that which remains.

Voice: Visualize your left foot. Are you your left foot?

You: No, I am not.

Voice: Visualize your left foot disappearing. If you had no left foot, would you still be you?

You: Yes. I am that which remains.

Voice: Are you your right leg?

You: No, I am not.

Voice: If you had no right leg, would you still be you?

You: Yes. I am that which remains.

Voice: Are you your left leg?

You: No, I am not.

Voice: If you had no left leg, would you still be you?

You: Yes. I am that which remains.

Voice: Are you the fingers of your right hand?

You: No, I am not.

Voice: If you had no fingers on your right hand, would you still be you?

You: Yes. I am that which remains.

Voice: Are you the fingers of your left hand?

You: No, I am not.

Voice: If you had no fingers on your left hand, would you still be you?

You: Yes. I am that which remains.

Voice: Are you your right hand?

You: No, I am not.

Voice: If you had no right hand, would you still be you?

You: Yes. I am that which remains.

Voice: Are you your right hand?

You: No, I am not.

Voice: If you had no right hand, would you still be you?

You: Yes. I am that which remains.

Voice: Are you your right arm?

You: No, I am not.

Voice: If you had no right arm, would you still be you?

You: Yes. I am that which remains.

Voice: Are you your sex organs?

You:	No, I am not.
Voice:	If you had no sex organs, would you still be you?
You:	Yes. I am that which remains.
Voice:	Are you your guts?
You:	No, I am not.
Voice:	If you had no guts, would you still be you?
You:	Yes. I am that which remains.
Voice:	Are you your lungs?
You:	No, I am not.
Voice:	If you had no lungs, would you still be you?
You:	Yes. I am that which remains.
Voice:	Are you your spine?
You:	No, I am not.
Voice:	If you had no spine, would you still be you?
You:	Yes. I am that which remains.
Voice:	Are you your heart?
You:	No, I am not.
Voice:	If you had no heart would you still be you?
You:	Yes. I am that which remains.
Voice:	Are you your eyes, your ears, your tongue?
You:	No, I am not.
Voice:	If you did not have your eyes, your ears, or your tongue, would you still be you?
You:	Yes. I am that which remains.
Voice:	Are you your brain?
You:	No, I am not.
Voice:	Then who *are* you?
You:	I am that which remains.

Pause for a moment and try to capture the essence of yourself as a disembodied consciousness that remains when all but you is gone. Then say aloud:

I am a light shining in the darkness.
I am the pure thought of the Divine.
I am the deathless center of all life.

When all else is gone,
I am that which remains.

The temple is closed.

Repeat the *body-dissolution/I am that which remains* meditation as much as possible. Each time, try to make the visualization clearer in your mind. Develop in your mind the clear reality of your continued, uninterrupted conscious existence even after all your body parts have disappeared.

Knowing you are you when you no longer have a physical body is the greatest magical power one can possess and the secret to overcoming death.

This exercise is worth a little practice.

PART II

Magical Weapons

FIVE

What Are the Magical Weapons, Really?

With the Wand createth He.
With the Cup preserveth He.
With the Dagger destroyeth He.
With the Coin redeemeth He.[13]

The Tarot card *the Magician* represents (among many other things) the alchemical element mercury, the planetary sphere of Mercury, the Roman god Mercury, the Greek god Hermes, and Thoth, the Egyptian god of magick. The classic image on the card shows the magician holding a wand high above his head with his right hand while he points downward with his left hand.

Before him is an altar or table upon which rest the *four primary weapons* of the magician:

---

13. Aleister Crowley, *The Holy Books of Thelema, Liber B vel Magi sub Figura I* (York Beach, ME: Samuel Weiser, 1983), p. 1.

- A *disk* (representing the element of earth, the material plane, the body, etc.)
- A *sword* (representing the element of air, the world of ideas, the mind and imagination, etc.)
- A *cup* (representing the element of water, the world of the soul intuition, the heart and emotions, etc.)
- A lance or *wand* (representing the element of fire, the world of pure will, the universal life force of the cosmos)

Magical weapons don't come ready-made. They have to be home-made or obtained and consecrated in a very personal and special manner. The traditional books of magick go to great lengths detailing precisely how to fashion each of these magical tools, and I've known quite a few magicians over the years who did a pretty good job following these an-cient recipes and made absolutely beautiful magical tools.

But I'm a pretty lazy guy and not at all handy, so I figure that just doing the best I can is … well … the best I *can do*. My homemade magi-cal weapons have served me well over the years, and as far as I'm con-cerned, they contain as much or more magical virtue than if they were actually Parsifal's lance, the Holy Grail, Excalibur, and the plate Jesus used to pass around canapés at the Last Supper.

Lazy or not, we all should take the greatest of interest in what our magical weapons are and how we go about bringing them into our lives. These simple objects represent all aspects of consciousness and being (and by that I mean *your* consciousness and the consciousness of the en-tire cosmos), organized into four broad categories. The qabalists identi-fied each of these four groupings with a letter from the Great Name, ‏ה ו‎ ‏ה י‎, one of the principal names of God found in the Old Testament: (Yod ‏י‎)–(Heh ‏ה‎)–(Vav ‏ו‎)–(Heh ‏ה‎), commonly pronounced *Jehovah*. Hebrew is written from right to left, so the Great Name is correctly written ‏יהוה‎.

I'm not going to delve deeply into qabalistic matters in this book, but I do want you to remember that, according to tradition, these four broad categories include the magician's **will** (Yod), **heart** (Heh), **mind** (Vav), and **body** (Heh), and that the four tools or weapons of the ma-gician represent these aspects of the magician's own being. They are solid, tangible, and objective articles—objects you can touch, pick up, wave about, and even taste. But they represent intangible (but very real), inward, subjective forces, powers, and principles—things most people can't even identify, let alone touch with their hands and fingers.

According to qabalistic tradition, humans are made in the "image" of deity, therefore the human soul is the miniature (microcosmic) reflection of the divine (macrocosmic) world. Both the *microcosm* and the *macrocosm* are divided into four categories: four macrocosmic worlds that are reflected in four microcosmic parts of the human soul. The concepts of these magical worlds and parts of the soul are neatly wrapped into four little bundles and turned into actual objects that are the four weapons of the magician.

י YOD—THE WAND

- In the macrocosm, Yod is Godhead itself.

- In the microcosm, Yod is the essence of the universal life force within each of us.

- Yod's magical weapon is the wand. No matter what material object you eventually use for your wand, you must have a spiritual connection to it. It must be as magically precious to you as if it had been personally placed in your hand by the Supreme Being itself.

ה HEH—THE CUP

- In the macrocosm, Heh is the archangelic world of titanic fundamental forces of nature.

- In the microcosm, Heh is the transcendent *soul intuition* within each of us.

- Heh's magical weapon is the cup. No matter what material object you eventually use for your cup, you must have a spiritual connection to it. It must be as magically precious to you as if it had been personally placed in your heart by a loving and breathtakingly beautiful archangel.

ו Vav—The Sword

- In the macrocosm, Vav is the angelic world of specific mechanical operations in nature.

- In the microcosm, Vav is our intellectual and reasoning process.

- Vav's magical weapon is the sword (or dagger). No matter what material object you eventually use for your sword, you must have a spiritual connection to it. It must be as magically precious to you as if it had been personally placed in your hand by a brilliant, beautiful, and fierce angel.

ה Heh—The Disk (or Pantacle)

- In the macrocosm, the final Heh is the material universe itself— matter and energy as manifested in the space-time dimension we perceive as "reality."

- In the microcosm, the final Heh includes our physical bodies.

- The final Heh's magical weapon is the disk or pantacle. No matter what material object you eventually use for your disk, you must have a spiritual connection to it. It must be as magically precious to you as if it had been personally placed in your hand by your own mother and father (idealized to perfection, of course).

SIX

The Magick Disk (or Pantacle)

Learn first—Oh thou who aspirest unto our ancient Order!—
that Equilibrium is the basis of the Work. If thou thyself hast not a
sure foundation, whereon wilt thou stand to direct the forces of Nature? [14]

I will start with the disk (or pantacle), as it represents the lowest rung on
the ladder of consciousness and is the first magical weapon the magician
creates in the opening act of his or her magical drama. It represents the
magician's perceived understanding of his or her immediate environment. It is the blueprint of the magician's *home*. It is *position*, the place the
magician first pretends to be at the beginning of the waking-up process.
It is *the firm foundation upon which we must stand to direct the forces of Nature.*

---

14. Aleister Crowley, *Magick: Liber ABA, Book Four—Liber Librae sub Figura XXX*
(York Beach, ME: Samuel Weiser, 1994), p. 668.

Just as your magical motto expresses *who* you are pretending to be, the disk expresses *where* you are pretending to be and where you are intending to go. The disk is your map. But it is a map you must draw yourself.

To start, you have to ask yourself, "Where do I think I am?"

I'm sorry to say, but it's impossible for you to know exactly where you are in the universe. Think about it. You're sitting somewhere reading this book. You probably don't even know precisely which way is east—and even if you do know, *what is* east, anyway? You're not exactly standing still. You're clinging to the surface of a sphere that is spinning over a thousand miles an hour, all the while you and the whole earth are being hurled at an unthinkable and variable speed around a star 93 million miles away, which along with you and me and the whole solar system is being dragged around some inscrutable center of our galaxy. Add to that the fact that the entire cosmos is expanding at an enormous speed away from an incomprehensible, pre-existent singularity.

Know where you are? Fat chance!

You have absolutely no idea where you are in the universe. Can you really be expected to know where your pretend self is positioned in the cosmos? The answer is simple: No! You can't!

But you've got to start somewhere. And to do that we have to first *pretend we know where we are.* This is why neophytes of the mysteries learn and regularly practice meditations and ceremonies like the rituals of the pentagram and hexagram that require us to presume that we are operating in a set position somewhere in the cosmos.

The pentagram rituals oblige us to move about as if we were positioned on the surface of the earth (an apparently *flat* earth) in the center of a circle demarcated by the four directions, north, south, east, and west. The pentagram rituals require the magician to become master of the local terrestrial (microcosmic) environment.

The hexagram rituals, on the other hand, work in the bigger world of the macrocosm and force the magician to expand his or her consciousness to encompass a larger universe—literally placing the magician as the sun surrounded by the belt of the zodiac. Both points of view are, of course, woefully inaccurate—but because you have to start somewhere, you put your *pretend self* in these *pretend locations*.

I learned these rituals very early on in my magical career because I was instructed by my teacher to do so. I really didn't know why I was practicing them. Only years later did it dawn on me what these exercises were doing to my consciousness and my *sense of position* in the universe. Think about it. When you visit a huge and crowded shopping mall, don't you always feel better when you find your location on the big *YOU ARE HERE* map? The tiny arrow points to a position on the map. Of course you are not actually there on that little arrow, but by mentally projecting yourself there, you become armed with a degree of knowledge and understanding that enables you to find your way around the mall. It also gives you an idea of your position and size in relationship to individual stores and the immensity of the mall.

As the magical weapon of the element of earth, the disk is your body and the spiritual food (bread) that sustains the body. It is the solid foundation upon which you will build your temple. It is also your *YOU ARE HERE* map. The disk is also called the pantacle, because the design that you create and engrave upon its surface will represent in symbolic form all [15] that you presently understand the universe to be.

Obviously, coming up with a design that symbolizes absolutely everything in your universe is a pretty tall order and requires a lot of thought and meditation. You need to do it, however, for unless you are "grounded" by the disk, you cannot begin the Great Work. The pantacle is your Yellow Brick Road, and you'll never get to the Emerald City to see the Wizard of Oz until you first find the Yellow Brick Road.

This is my pantacle (see illustration).

---

15. *Pan* is Greek for "all" and also the root for "bread" in Latin and Romance languages.

The Pantacle of Frater L.M.D.

I designed it in August of 1976 following my First Degree initiation[16] in the O.T.O. My inspiration was a combination of Thelemic and qabalistic clichés; therefore, the terms I use when describing the universal principles I'm representing are those commonly used by magicians who subscribe to the magick of Aleister Crowley's Thelema. Other magicians of different spiritual backgrounds can and should work with the exact same images and concepts but describe them with terms from their own traditions, such as Hindu, Buddhist, Christian, Jewish, Islamic, etc.

My pantacle has served me well up to this point in my magical career. I can't seem to come up with a better one, unlike with my motto. All aspects of my understanding of my (for lack of a better word) "reality" continue to be represented to my satisfaction on this figure. Here is a description of it in a nutshell. As you read it, try to understand what I was trying to do with the design, then think about how you will represent your understanding of the universe on your pantacle.

---

16. Technically, the O.T.O.'s "First Degree" is the second initiation into the Order. Prior to this is a "Zero Degree" preliminary ritual (Minerval). I received my Minerval initiation on November 15, 1975, E.V. My First Degree took place on August 14, 1976, E.V. in Dublin, California. Presiding officers were Grady L. McMurtry, IX°–X°, Phyllis Seckler McMurtry, IX°, and Helen Parsons Smith, IX°.

THE PANTACLE OF FRATER L.M.D.

The basic format of my pantacle was suggested to me by something I read in Crowley's *Magick: Liber ABA, Book IV, part II:*[17]

> *The Wand was the Will of man, his wisdom, his word; the Cup was his understanding, the vehicle of grace; the Sword was his reason; and the Pantacle shall be his body, the Temple of the Holy Ghost.*
>
> *What is the length of this Temple?*
>
> *From North to South.*
>
> *What is the breadth of this Temple?*
>
> *From East to West.*
>
> *What is the height of this Temple?*
>
> *From Abyss to Abyss.*
>
> *…All Pantacles will contain the ultimate conceptions of the circle and the cross…the Tree of Life itself may be figured therein…the Pantacle will be imperfect unless each idea is contrasted in a balanced manner with its opposite, and unless there is a necessary connection between each pair of ideas and every other pair.*

I first and foremost wanted my pantacle to represent three absolutes: the absolute *biggest thing* in the universe, the absolute *smallest thing* in the universe, and absolutely *everything in between* those two absolutes. Let's talk about the rim of my pantacle first.

The first two "ultimate conceptions" in my magical reality are two infinities: the infinite *out* and the infinite *in*. The infinite out is the outer limits of our expanding universe—quite literally, the outermost reaches of expanding space. In the specific language of Thelemic cosmology, this huge infinity is identified as the goddess Nuit (also spelled Nuith), the Egyptian sky goddess whose very body is the starry universe. You can't get any bigger or more *outer-er* than that! I chose to acknowledge this aspect of my universe on my pantacle by placing the name *NUITH* on the circumference.

---

17. Aleister Crowley, *Magick: Liber ABA, Book Four—Liber Librae sub Figura XXX* (York Beach, ME: Samuel Weiser, 1994), pp. 95–97.

Furthermore, because "the Pantacle will be imperfect unless each idea is contrasted in a balanced manner with its opposite," I chose to also acknowledge upon the rim of my pantacle the opposite infinity. (Yes, there can be two infinities.) Because the circumference (Nuith) is in a very real sense everywhere, so too must be the theoretical center of this everywhere-ness. This tiny infinite *in-ness* is identified as the god Hadit (also spelled Hadith), the infinite point in the very center, the heart, of the body of Nuit.

Because Nuit is the infinite out and Hadit is the infinite in, they are both infinitely everywhere—infinitely touching and rubbing and caressing—the infinite heart of Hadit beating eternally in the infinite center of the body of Nuit. This is cosmic lovemaking on unimaginably large *and* minute scales, and results in the birth of an infinite baby, the child of Nuit and Hadit.

The child is the creative vibration generated by the friction of the universal in uniting with the universal out. This ecstatic vibration creates the field of operation (mass, matter, and energy) upon which (and within which) the entire universe actually manifests in space-time. In the nomenclature of Thelemic magick, the child is called *Ra-Hoor-Khuit*. I placed his name not on the outer perimeter of the pantacle, with his infinitely abstract and unmanifest parents, but on the *inside* of the perimeter of the pantacle—to illustrate the manifest nature of this field of operation. Nuit is the biggest thing in the universe, Hadit is the smallest thing in the universe, and Ra-Hoor-Khuit provides the foundation for absolutely everything in between.

The cross is the next major feature of my pantacle. Just as Hadit is at the center of Nuit's body, I placed a small circle in the very center of the disk. For me this represents the first "One" of manifest creation. In qabalistic terms, it is Godhead, the Crown, Kether, the first emanation of the Tree of Life.

*The Infinite "Out" (Nuith), the Infinite "In" (Hadith),
and Their Infinite Point of Contact (Ra-Hoor-Khuit)*

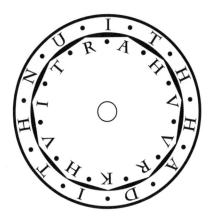

*Infinities Concentrated into the Primal Singularity—
Kether on the Qabalistic Tree of Life*

What is the length of this Temple?
From North to South.
What is the breadth of this Temple?
From East to West.

This point is the primal One—Kether—the Crown, from which emanate the other sephiroth of the Tree of Life. But there are four Trees of Life representing the four qabalistic worlds (Atziluth, Briah, Yetzirah, and Assiah) and the four parts of the soul. The cross of my pantacle is made from four Trees of Life bursting in the four directions from the primal Kether. This way of looking at things shows a total of thirty-seven[18] sephiroth.

The Four Qabalistic Worlds and the Four Parts of the Soul
All Emanating from the Primal Singularity

What is the height of this Temple?
From Abyss to Abyss.

I now draw your attention to the black eleven-sided abyss between the perimeter and the central field, and the black circle abyss that backs the supernal triads of the four Trees of Life. These abysses (which are really one ... really none!) guard the two border areas of being: (1) being

---

18. Thirty-seven is the number of the Hebrew word *Jechidah,* describing the ultimate unity of the soul.

coming forth from unmanifest potentiality, and (2) fully realized being returning to unmanifest potentiality.

Even if you don't follow my thinking on these qabalistic matters, I hope you get the general idea of what I was trying to achieve with my pantacle. On my map, I can point out specific landmarks of creation and consciousness as I understand them: fundamental forces of nature, parts of the soul, qabalistic worlds, elements, planets and planetary spheres, zodiac signs, even Tarot cards and initiatory grades.

Now it's your turn. What does your universe look like? It could be as profoundly simple as the yin-yang symbol, a pentagram, or a square and a triangle. But you must ask yourself if you will be able to point out exactly where on that simple symbol you could find, for example, the sun, or the element of air, or the zodiac sign Capricorn. What combination of words, symbols, and figures do you need to assemble to represent your idea of infinite space or exactly where you could pinpoint your present degree of initiation of illumination? Where is the next step in your spiritual evolution?

As with your magical motto, you will probably make several (perhaps *many*) different pantacles during your long and illustrious magical career. But you have to start somewhere, and you have to start some time. That time is now.

I would like you to create your own homemade magick pantacle in the blank disk on the next page. Sign it with your own magical motto. Give it some thought, but remember that your understanding of your universe is changing with every breath you take. You will most likely change the design many times in the future, so don't take too much time now. There's no time like the present, so do it now!

The Magick Pantacle of _____

....

.... *(date)*

ACTUALLY MAKING A PANTACLE

I probably should apologize for rambling on and on about the importance of the *design* for your pantacle without offering any practical advice as to how you might go about making the material object itself. Let's change that right now. Here are a few thoughts and suggestions.

Using standards set by the Golden Dawn, the pantacle should be eight inches in diameter and half an inch thick. It should be round, flat, and rather heavy—*round*, because it should remind you of both the ring of the horizon that surrounds you as you stand on the surface of the earth *and* the disk of the sun that circles you daily in the heavens; *flat*, because your work must be built upon a foundation that is level; and *heavy*, because the magician's work must be firmly and substantially grounded and (for the time being at least) fixed in place.

If the pantacle is made of metal, the ideal material is gold or gold-plated silver. Not many of us today can afford a round slab of pure gold eight inches in diameter and half an inch thick, so this is not an option for most magicians.

Beeswax is also an ideal material for a pantacle and has been used for centuries by magicians. Not only is beeswax infinitely more inexpensive than gold or indeed any metal, but it is very easy (indeed, pleasurable) to work with. It smells wonderful, too. If cared for properly, it will last hundreds of years. It is the product of industrious labor and is actually a living substance. Among its many other attributes, the pantacle represents the magician's livelihood and material sustenance. It is quite literally the *food* of the magician. When one looks at one's pantacle, one should feel a visceral urge to take a bite out of it—like eating the earth … like eating the sun … like eating the body of God. A pantacle of beeswax fills the bill nicely!

Beeswax is easy to obtain, if you know where to look. Most farmers' markets have at least one honey farmer (apiarist) who also sells blocks of beeswax. It is also found in bulk at hardware stores, where it is sold as a bolt and screw lubricant. Food grade, however, is preferable. Candle wax or paraffin is also easy to obtain and, while less desirable from a mystical perspective, is very easy to work with.

Paraffin candle stubs are in no short supply at the DuQuette house. For many years we celebrated the Gnostic Mass in our living room at least once a month. The high altar of the lovely ceremony was illuminated by twenty-two candles, which we replaced after two or three usages. I have used recycled mass candles to make several versions of my personal pantacle, my Enochian magick sigillum, and assorted other magick disks.

Directions for Making a Homemade Wax Pantacle

1. Find or buy a round biscuit tin or Christmas cookie tin approximately eight inches in diameter (a little more or less will be fine). Clean it thoroughly, then coat the inside with cooking oil spray or vegetable oil. You will *not* be using the lid to the tin.

2. Place your blocks of beeswax, paraffin, or candle stubs inside the container. (Estimate and use your own judgment as to how much

wax it will take, so that when melted, the disk will be approximately half an inch thick.)

3. Place the biscuit tin with wax on a cookie sheet.

4. Making sure none of the blocks of wax or candle stubs lean over the rim of the container, place the tin in your kitchen oven at a very low temperature.

5. WATCH THE MELTING EVERY MINUTE! Do not leave the room for a moment! Keep checking to make sure the wax is melting and not leaking onto the cookie sheet or the floor of the oven. At the first signs of leaking, remove everything immediately and turn off the oven. (I'm being so insistent about safety because *I once set fire to the house doing this*. It wasn't pretty! Constance is still upset.)

6. Be patient. Everything will eventually melt into a beautiful liquid wax.

7. Carefully remove the tin from the oven and allow to cool slowly at room temperature. Do not try to hurry the cooling process by placing the tin in the refrigerator or freezer, as you will risk cracking the wax.

8. After the wax has cooled completely to room temperature (at least four hours), turn the tin over and gently slam it on the countertop. If you oiled the tin sufficiently, a perfect wax disk will pop right out. The "bottom" will become the perfectly smooth "top" surface of your disk.

9. Apply your pantacle's design with a sharp-pointed object such as a compass point.

Hints for Carving Your Design on a Wax Disk

- First, draw your design on a sheet of paper. The drawing can be eight inches in diameter, but you will want to make several photocopies of it, and the photocopies should be enlarged (or reduced) to perfectly match the size of your wax disk.

- When you are ready to begin, cut out your paper drawing of the disk and secure it to the wax disk with several pieces of tape.

- Then, using a thin sewing needle, pierce every place on your drawing where a line (1) starts, (2) ends, and (3) intersects another line. Make sure the perforations go completely through the paper and lightly into the wax. THIS CAN TAKE A LONG TIME. Be patient and careful.

- When you are absolutely certain you have marked every landmark on your design, remove the paper and, using your compass point and a straight edge, draw your design on the surface of the wax.

- For the lettering, you will have to more or less eyeball it and do the best you can. If you take your time and are careful, you will be rewarded with the most beautiful object of art you have ever created ... and it will truly be your magick pantacle.

PANTACLE FOR THE IMPATIENT, LAZY, INEPT, OR HOPELESSLY AWKWARD MAGICIAN

If working with beeswax or paraffin seems beyond your artistic skill level but you still want to create a bona fide magick pantacle, you can do this:

1. Go to an arts and crafts or hobby store and buy a round wooden disk, such as those manufactured for plaques, photo mounting, etc.

2. Lightly sand, smooth, and brush clean the disk.

3. Take a photocopy of your design (carefully trimmed to fit handsomely to the wooden disk) and spray the back of the paper with spray adhesive (available at the crafts store).

4. Carefully adhere the paper drawing to the wood, being careful to avoid bubbles.

5. Let dry overnight.

6. Following the directions on the can, spray or brush-seal the disk, front and back, with a clear commercial glossy or semi-glossy finisher. Ask for suggestions at the crafts store where you bought your wooden disk.

IDEAS FOR AN ON-THE-ROAD, IMPROVISED HOMEMADE PANTACLE

Once you've designed and constructed your pantacle, you will have in essence installed it permanently in your magical self. That's where it truly exists. That's where you use it. From that point on, any material object you choose to be your pantacle *is* your pantacle. It's desirable, however, that it be round like the disk of the sun and suggestive of the solid and nutritive spiritual attributes of earth.

I travel a lot and often find myself quietly doing magick in hotel rooms and in the guestrooms of friends and colleagues. I don't usually travel with my formal, consecrated magical tools, so I improvise with what is at hand.

Here are a few things I've used on the road for my magick pantacle:

- A coin
- The Ace of Disks Tarot card
- My wristwatch
- A round cocktail coaster from a pub or hotel bar
- A tiny packet of salt from a cafe or restaurant
- A CD or DVD
- A tortilla, pita bread, or pancake (really!)

SEVEN

The Magick Sword

The Magick Sword is the analytical faculty ... attributed to air, all-wandering, all-penetrating, but unstable ... The Sword, necessary as it is to the Beginner, is but a crude weapon. Its function is to keep off the enemy or to force a passage through them—and though it must be wielded to gain admission to the palace it cannot be worn to the wedding feast.[19]

The pantacle is engraved with a *symbol* that represents the magician's universe. The sword bears a *word* that represents the magician's universe. This can actually be a word (a noun, pronoun, verb, adverb, adjective, preposition, conjunction, or interjection in some language that is meaningful to you) engraved upon the blade of an actual sword. Or the "word" of the sword can be a more subtle vibratory expression of your universe than that which can be articulated by sounds originating in your meat larynx and pushed over your flapping tongue and out your mouth.

19. Aleister Crowley, *Magick: Liber ABA, Book Four—Liber Librae sub Figura XXX* (York Beach, ME: Samuel Weiser, 1994), p. 86.

I would like to be able to tell you that I made my magick sword my-self—that I, like the ancient magicians, dug the ore out of the ground with a shovel I had fashioned myself; that I smelted the ore (in the heat of charcoal I made from the wood of a tree I had planted myself as a young boy and then chopped down myself); that I hammered the raw metal into a blade, etc. I'd like to be able to share with you the secret magick word I engraved upon its shining blade: "Shazam!" "Abracadab-ra!" "Etteuqud!" But I didn't do any of those things.

I bought my magick sword at an antique store near my home in Costa Mesa, California. But before you chastise me for being lazy and unmagical, I would like to share with you the circumstances surround-ing its acquisition and what my magick sword means to me—how it qualifies to be my word. Hopefully the story will give you some idea of what these homemade magical weapons are truly about, and what you will need to do to create or earn yours.

My sword is a beautiful, but modest, Masonic Knights Templar cer-emonial sword made in the United States sometime between 1893 and 1923. There are thousands of them still cluttering the walls of antique stores and attics all over the world, and if you are lucky you can prob-ably still find one for yourself for less than a hundred dollars.

I had been shopping for a good ceremonial sword ever since I was made Master of Heru-ra-ha Lodge, O.T.O., in January of 1978. Not only is a lightweight sword a necessary tool used in all the O.T.O.'s degree initiation ceremonies, but it is also the weapon of the Priestess in the Gnostic Mass, the Order's publicly celebrated ritual. In other words, both Constance and I need a good sword in the house.

I located the sword of my dreams at a local antique store. It was a Masonic Knights Templar Commander's sword, in good shape (for some-thing at least eighty years old) and adorned with esoteric symbols that are just as appropriate to ceremonial magick as they are to Freemasonry. It was the perfect length and weight and came with its original scabbard, also beautifully and appropriately adorned. It was reasonably priced, but at the time I didn't have the money to buy it. In fact, I didn't have money to buy much of anything.

Looking back, I'm happy that I didn't have the funds to just pur-
chase it when I first saw it in the shop, because if I had just thrown it
in my shopping cart, that particular sword might never have gotten itself infused with much magick. But I'll get to that part of the story in
a moment. I need to tell you that my magick sword didn't start out as a
sword. First, it was a guitar—a very special guitar.

It was a handsome instrument—the finest I'd ever owned—a 1968
C.F. Martin D-28 with a butter-smooth setup and rich response that
was just perfect for my (then) primitive rhythm accompaniment style.
I selected it from out of a dozen high-end guitars I sampled at Johnny
Thompson Music, the legendary store in El Monte, California, that ser-
viced the artists and bands that populated the touring and recording cul-
ture of that golden age of popular music. Our producer at Epic Records
drove my partner Charley[20] and me there one afternoon in early 1970
and told us, "Pick out whatever you want!"

I loved that guitar and broke it in writing songs and recording two
singles, an album, and playing more live performances than my hashish-
addled years of sex, drugs, and rock 'n' roll will permit me to remember.

A friend and guitar student of mine, who happened to be a master
woodworker, begged me to allow him (for an insanely reasonable price)
to inlay the neck and headstock with mother-of-pearl and abalone shell.
He adorned the fret markers with generous double triangles of mother-of-pearl, and at the twelfth fret he placed the Roman numeral XCIII
(93)[21] in iridescent green, blue, and pink abalone shell. On the headstock
he inlaid in abalone shell the name "C. F. Martin," which plunged proud-
ly between the rows of gold Schaller™ tuning posts.

The crowning glory of my sweet Martin was the inlaid Egyptian
winged solar disk centered at the top of the headstock. Every feather
was a separate iridescent piece of mother-of-pearl or abalone shell cut
and ground individually at a different angle and polished so it caught and

---

20. Charley D. & Milo, Epic Records, BMI, 1970.

21. Ninety-three is a particularly "magical" number, especially to magicians who
embrace or are influenced by the philosophy known as Thelema. *Thelema*, a
Greek word meaning "will," enumerates numerically to 93.

reflected light from a different direction. As the guitar moved under the stage lights, the feathers appeared to flutter and dazzled the eye.

Did I say it was a handsome guitar? It was breathtaking—my most precious possession, the apple of my eye and ear. It was coveted by every guitarist who laid eyes on it. In my mind, that guitar, more than anything else—more than my songs, more than my live performances, more than my own talent (real or imagined), even more than my recording career—defined who and what I was as an artist. It was my Excalibur.

But in December of 1978, magick had become my art. I no longer made my living on stage and in the studio. I had over-enjoyed the excesses of the aspiring rock star. I was a married man with a beautiful wife and little son (born in 1972), and in spite of the wild and wonderful adventures I had experienced on the road, I really *did* want to be a good husband and stable father. The alcohol, the drugs, and the ladies ultimately couldn't compete with the love and warmth of my little family.

For several years after I said goodbye to music, I worked a string of low-paying technical positions in the medical device manufacturing industry. The jobs barely paid the rent on our little apartment in Costa Mesa, and there was very little left over every month for food. I must confess, the DuQuettes owed our existence to the almost supernatural thriftiness of my dear wife, Constance.

Christmas that year fell on a Monday. The company I was working for gave us only one day off for the holiday. Management waited until the end of the day on Friday, December 22, to announce that regrettably there would be no Christmas bonuses or year-end gifts for the hourly employees.

Even though the DuQuettes are not Christian, our family loves the Christmas season and makes the most of the cultural celebration. That year Constance had brought home an inexpensive little tree (strapped to her bicycle). It was gaily decorated and had been emanating its Jovian perfume into our tiny living room for over a week. A handful of small, homemade gifts were already wrapped and under the tree, but the *real gifts* I was planning to get for Constance and little Jean-Paul had yet to be purchased—awaiting the Christmas bonus money that was not going to come. I felt pretty much like Bob Cratchit in Dickens's *A Christ-*

mas Carol, faced with the grim prospect of delivering bad news to his family on Christmas Eve.

I sat in my little cubical at work and wallowed for a few minutes in self-pity. It was not a very dignified attitude for someone who was starting to identify himself as a serious magician. In fact, I didn't feel like much of a magician at all. Poverty had dogged us from the moment I abandoned my recording career in 1972. My *real-world* jobs to this point had served to barely keep our heads above water. I was hoping that this Christmas would be different—a cheery and festive occasion for Constance and little Jean-Paul—like the Christmases my hardworking parents had managed to throw for my brother and me in the 1950s.

It then occurred to me that I had one asset, one golden treasure that I might sacrifice on the altar of Christmas to save the day: my Martin. Even without the custom inlay work, it was easily worth a thousand dollars. I didn't, however, have time to find a buyer to give me close to what it was worth. It was too precious an item to pawn for just a few dollars, so I set the insanely low figure of three hundred fifty dollars (the amount I had estimated my bonus would have been) and resolved that if I could immediately get that much money for the instrument, I would sell it and go Christmas shopping.

I swung by our apartment after work and picked up my precious D-28, then drove directly to Coast Music in Costa Mesa. They knew me there. During our recording years, Charley and I were local "Hollywood" recording-star celebrities. The owner also knew my guitar and was forever suggesting that I sell it to him.

Late as it was in the day, the store was still full of customers, mostly professional musicians shopping for supplies for holiday gigs. The owner was happy to see me and lamented the fact that I hadn't been in for a while. I laid the guitar case on the display case and said flatly, "I'm selling my Martin."

He looked surprised and genuinely sad. Still, there was a glint of greed in his eyes. "Are you sure about this?" was his first response. I nodded in the affirmative.

He sighed and started to open the case. "Okay, I'll write it up and put it on consignment. What's your asking price?"

"I don't want to put it on consignment," I told him. "I want to sell it to *you*—right now—for three hundred fifty dollars in cash."

He looked at me in complete disbelief. He flared his nostrils in a not-so-subtle attempt to sniff out alcohol or drugs on my breath. "I can't do this, Lon. Give this some thought."

"I've given it a lot of thought. It's Christmas Eve. I need three hundred fifty dollars for the family's Christmas."

He closed the case and said, "Sorry, man. I couldn't live with myself. It's your baby. You don't want to do this."

"Okay," I said. "If it will make you feel better, you can give me the money and throw in a replacement guitar from off the wall."

He thought for a moment and said, "Okay!" He then walked over to the wall display of guitars and picked out a beautiful new Gibson J-45. "Will this do?"

"Sure," I said. "If it will make you feel better."

A Gibson J-45 is a pretty fine instrument and represented an extremely generous trade. A few minutes later, I walked out of the store with three hundred fifty dollars in cash and a new guitar. I headed straight to the antique store and purchased two items: a rocking chair Constance had admired and my magick sword. Constance and I spent the rest of the magick cash at the toy store.

In the spring, I sold the Gibson to a friend, and for the next twenty-nine years, I didn't own or play a guitar. I left the world of music and embarked on the study and practice of ceremonial magick and the associated arts. My sword—my store-bought, inexpensive Masonic ceremonial blade—has gotten quite a workout in the last forty years. I wouldn't dream of trading it in for a new one. It is my Excalibur, my Sting, my Nothung. I carry it in dreams and visions. With it, I have done battle with the dragons of my own nightmares, banished demons, and stormed the gates of heaven. My cheap Masonic sword is the material metaphor of my *word*. I needed it to find my voice, the voice of my own Great Work for which my old Martin guitar was merely a pre-echo.

With my sword, I banished the demons of indolence and laziness, invoked the gods of discipline and focus, and pierced the mysteries of my own soul until I cut through and found my magical voice—the *word* of my own Great Work. Every word I write—every sentence, every poem, every book that pours onto the page—is my *word*. My sword is my tongue, my keyboard, my computer, my printer, my telephone, my network of Brothers and Sisters, friends and colleagues.

What is your *word*? The answer to that question will hand you your magick sword. It's likely you will try out many lesser swords before you find the true one. But once again, you have to start *somewhere*, and there's no time like the present. But before I give you a bit of sword-shopping advice, I'd like to share the latest episode in my magick sword adventure.

It seems that my magick has come full circle. My original magick sword has come back to me—as surely as if it had been returned newly forged from the hand of the Lady of the Lake. No, my old Martin D-28 didn't reappear miraculously on my doorstep. But something almost as amazing happened.

A couple years ago, after a break of thirty-five years, I started writing songs again. It seemed like a natural evolution of my writing and magical career. I'd been lucky to secure a song publisher and record label, and I really enjoyed playing a few songs at my talks and workshops. Shortly before my sixty-fifth birthday, I entered one of my newly recorded songs in a national songwriting competition. I shamelessly appealed to my family, friends, colleagues, and social-network contacts to listen to it and (if they absolutely didn't *hate* it) vote for it. When the contest ended and the votes were counted, I won first place. The prize? A beautiful new (and rather expensive) Alvarez Masterworks *guitar*.

Making (or Selecting) Your Homemade Sword

As I confessed earlier, I do not have the skill or the wherewithal to fabricate a proper sword. If you are blessed with those skills, or if you know someone who is, I encourage you to think long and hard about the design of both the blade and handle, then commence or commission the project.

If you resolve to buy or obtain an existing manufactured sword (which is probably what most modern magicians must do), here are a few ideas that might be helpful:

- Keep in mind that your magick sword is a *ceremonial* sword. If it is too large or heavy, you will not be able to hold it up for the long periods of time that are often necessary, especially in spirit evocations. An oversized sword will defeat you faster than the most dangerous demon.

- For symbolic reasons, a double-edged blade is preferable to one with a single edge. This is a sword after all, not a big knife, ax, hatchet, or machete. Even a letter opener–type dagger is preferable to a knife. Your sword should come to a point at the end; however, neither the tip nor the edges should be dangerously sharp. This is a symbolic weapon. The foes you will be conjuring, battling, banishing, and intimidating with the sword are spiritual adversaries and not flesh and blood. You will also likely be using your sword in group ceremonies, often in small, cramped temple spaces. Over the years I've been in too many ceremonies that were interrupted by *accidental* injuries inflicted by "magicians" brandishing razor-sharp "ceremonial" swords. It is very awkward explaining to an ambulance driver why your bleeding "house guest" is wearing a black, hooded robe!

- When shopping for your sword, pay attention to how it is balanced in your hand. You will feel an indescribable pleasure and a powerful sense of confidence in the deepest recesses of your soul when you pick up a perfectly balanced sword. Pick up a thousand swords if you have to until you feel that power. When you do, that's your sword.

Ideas for an On-the-Road, Improvised Homemade Sword

Once you've designed and made (or obtained) your sword, you will have in essence installed it permanently in your magical self. That's where it truly exists. That's where you use it. From that point on, any material object you choose to be your sword *is* your sword. It's desirable, however, that it be somewhat "sword-like" or evocative of the spiritual attributes of air.

Here are a few things I've used on the road for my magick sword:

- A plastic cocktail sword. (Yes, the kind the bartender sticks through olives and cocktail onions. Granted, it's a little small, but in a pinch it works great!)

- A hotel silverware knife.

- A fan. (A magick fan, the instrument of air, is the Eastern equivalent of the sword. A viable fan can be made in seconds by folding and pleating a sheet of paper or, better yet, the laminated card stock of hotel room-service menus.)

- I always pack a tiny switchblade knife that looks like a miniature dagger when the blade is out.

EIGHT

The Magick Cup

The magick of the cup comes not from its form or its beauty
or the material from which it is composed. The magick of the cup
simply comes from its ability to embody profound and perfect emptiness.

The magick cup is the magician's *understanding*—not so much the active intellectual understanding (which is the function of the sword), but the profound and passive understanding of the heart—an understanding that transcends the reasoning processes. It is through this understanding that the magician's work is purified. The cup is the first letter *H* (Heh ה) in the Great Name: *Yod Heh Vav Heh,* הוהי. It represents the element of water and the second-highest aspect of the human soul, the "soul intuition."[22]

It is impossible to properly comment on the nature of the cup without also discussing the wand. Indeed, the cup and wand are a team, supreme cosmic lovers—the wand the ultimate active, positive projection of light, energy, and love, and the cup the ultimate passive, negative receptacle of

---

22. The neshamah.

all light, energy, and love. If we were to use familiar astronomical allusions, the wand is the sun, which projects and radiates light, and the cup is the moon, which passively receives and reflects the sun's light. Continuing with that theme, the wand is all galaxies of stars, and the cup is the infinite womb of space itself.

If we were to speak in religious terms, the wand is the active process of worship, of chanting or of prayer, while the cup is the still, silent waiting for deity's response after the worship. Formal magical ceremonies usually begin with cleansing of the temple. This is done with water from the cup. Even before the magician starts the ceremony, he or she bathes in pure water and puts on clean vestments. The cleansing of the body and clothes is a function of the cup.

Christians are initially baptized, and Muslims perform Wudu before praying in the mosque. Jews of old were fully immersed in the mikvah pool outside the temple, and many initiatory societies ritualistically bathe the candidates for initiation. The magician sees all these gestures of purification as the function of the magick cup, and without a cup the magician is just not ready to do business.

Obviously all this translates neatly into the familiar allegories of human sexuality and all the wondrous issues that accompany the concepts of physical and emotional love. For us, sex is the clearest, simplest magical metaphor for the mechanics of creation, and the cup represents the female aspect in everything … in *everyone*.

Making (or Selecting) Your Homemade Cup

Once again, I confess that I did not make my own magick cup. I just don't have the skill or resources to fashion a viable cup. My cup is a simple stemmed brass chalice that was given to me as a gift from a dear friend on the eve of the very first Gnostic Mass that Constance and I celebrated in 1978. We have used it for every mass since. I can think of no more sacred, magical, or precious cup for me to use in magical ceremonies.

You could say I am in the process of perpetually consecrating my cup. For me, this process is the essence and the power of the cup, so I would like to take a bit of space in this book to share what exactly that means to me. I hope it will help with your *understanding* of what your cup can mean to you in your magical journey.

As I just mentioned, my cup is a simple brass chalice. Brass tarnishes easily and quickly, so each time I intend to use my cup, I must first polish it to pristine brilliance. You might think that taking time to polish brass prior to every magical operation is an inconvenience—and you'd be right. It's a real pain! I grumble out loud as I dodge the deadly black-widow spiders in the garage as I search for the brass polish and rags and newspapers and paper towels.

The brass cleaner is nasty and toxic, which is why Constance makes me keep it in the infernal depths of the garage. It stinks so strongly, I have to do my polishing on the patio in the backyard. I don't dare wear any clothes that I ever intend to wear again, so I strip down to just a pair of old swimming trunks (even in the bitter Southern California winters). I'm sure the neighbors over the fence must be disgusted at the sight of a crabby, half-naked old wizard muttering to himself, but I don't care. Once I begin, I just want to get the job over with. I've got magick to do!

I vigorously shake the can of brass polish, pop off the crusty lid, and soak my rag with a generous dose of the caramel-colored liquid. I slather my cup inside and out with that vile-smelling poison and start to rub it in. Everything on the surface of the cup almost immediately turns black, a sign that the chemicals are working on the brass.

Then, just like clockwork, my whole attitude changes. I become focused. I become inspired. I actually start to enjoy my work. I see my labor for what it really is—a magical operation, a consecration ceremony. This is not a household chore. It is alchemy, prayer, worship, devotion, adoration, *love*.

Every smudge, every stain, and every lip mark and fingerprint left on the metal from the vicissitudes of my last magical operation—my last *incarnation*—I now see as the traces of so many karmic debts, stains upon my soul; stains that I can now wipe away with the polish of my devotion, my love, my *understanding*.

I change rags and start to wipe away the excess polish. As my cup slowly turns from black to gold, I begin to take an almost obsessive interest in buffing away every blemish. I turn the cup over and over in my hands, seeking out any remnant of past laziness, selfishness, thoughtless-ness—anything that could have left its shameful smear upon my beloved cup. Some marks are very stubborn, so I have to reapply the polish sev-eral times.

My fingers are now black. The cuticles of my fingernails have become blackened crescent moons, but finally my beautiful cup (now warm from the friction of my ardor) mirrors in immaculate detail the golden glory of the sun. In those few moments, I have become the soot-blackened Vulcan-Hephaestus clumsily caressing in my brutish hands the delicate pink body of my bride Venus.

I stop polishing only when I *understand* in my soul that I now hold in my hands the Holy Grail itself—until I *understand* that when I put this sacred vessel to my lips I will be drinking the Life of the Sun, the Elixir of Life, and the Dew of Immortality.

YOUR MAGICK CUP

Not everyone is as inept as I am in the workshop. You might be more handy with metal or wood or glass and have all the necessary resources to fashion your own cup from scratch. If so, you might want to look at a few images of examples of magick cups that are found in abundance on the Internet. One classic example of a magick cup has a triangular base, a spherical center stem, and a crescent moon for a bowl.

Because of its association with the moon and water, silver is a most appropriate metal for a magick cup. But glass, brass, pewter, and wood are also popular materials. Blues, silvers, and sea greens are perfect colors.

Even though I've never made a cup myself, a friend of ours described how her husband once made one himself. Before her death in 2003, the DuQuettes were privileged to be friends with Helen Parsons Smith, the widow of two great American magicians, Jack Parsons and Wilfred Smith. Helen told us how Jack had made his own crude cup.

He purchased two very thin sheets of pure silver, one perfectly round, about eight inches in diameter, and the other square, about five inches square. He took the round piece of silver to a beach in Malibu and laid it on the wet sand at the water's edge. He then carefully proceeded to pound the center of the disk with a wooden pestle. It took quite a long time, but eventually he beat the round disk into a semblance of the bowl of a cup. Back in his home workshop, he used a jeweler's saw to cut three identical crescent "moons" from the square piece of silver. Once those were cleaned and polished, he soldered the moons to the sides of the bowl to form three legs. Simple, beautiful, and he did it all himself.

IDEAS FOR AN ON-THE-ROAD, IMPROVISED HOMEMADE CUP

About ten years ago, I was speaking in Oslo and had need of a magick cup for a magical operation I intended to perform the following evening. I was staying with friends, and my "temple" was the guestroom of their home. Before retiring, I performed the water section of the *Preliminary Invocation of the Goetia*[23] with the object of locating an appropriate "travel" magick cup. No sooner had I concluded the ritual than my host knocked on the door of my room and announced we would be visiting the Vigeland Sculpture Park in the morning.

The park is one of the most breathtakingly beautiful places I have ever seen. I toured with about a dozen local lodge members who had all been there many times. Before we headed home, we all wanted to visit the gift shop. A young lady from our party called my name and motioned me over to an exhibit of tiny pewter wine cups, replicas of ancient Norwegian ritual cups. My face lit up, and she sensed that I liked them very much. "I buy one for you," she said. I made a most insincere and feeble attempt at protest. It has been my travel cup ever since.

Once you've designed and made (or obtained) your cup, you will have in essence installed it permanently in your magical self. That's where it truly exists. That's where you use it. From that point on, any material receptacle you choose to be your cup *is* your cup. It's desirable, however, that it be somewhat "cup-like" and evocative of the spiritual attributes of water.

---

23. The *Preliminary Invocation of the Goetia* is a classic ritual of ceremonial magick that is used to invoke and charge one's temple and/or magical implements with the powers and virtues of the elements: fire, water, air, earth, and spirit.

Here are a few things I've used on the road for my magick cup:

- A wine or cocktail glass
- A coffee cup
- A bottle
- A bottle cap
- A tree leaf
- A nutshell
- A gourd
- A rose
- My own cupped hand

NINE

The Magick Wand

Touch me with your hazel wand.
Fill my soul with light.
Bring me from darkness into light.
CHARLEY D. & MILO [24]

The magician who is also a qabalist will probably be happy to babble on to you about how the magick wand represents the sacred element of fire;[25] how it is the magical weapon that represents Atziluth, the archetypal world,

---

24. "Touch Me with Your Hazel Wand," Charles D. Harris and Lon Milo Du-Quette (Charley D. & Milo), Epic Records/Hazelwand Publishing, 1968.

25. The traditions of Paganism associate the athame (dagger or sword) with fire and the phallus principle, and the wand with air and the intellect. Indeed, the dramatic climax of the overtly sexual Great Rite of the Witches celebrates the union of male and female, sun and moon, fire and water, by penetrating a cup with the athame. All symbolism is ultimately arbitrary, of course, but in my mind there is a visceral disconnect here. The dagger is a weapon of injury that stabs, slices, cuts, and severs flesh. Naturally, such a weapon penetrates the flesh, but in my mind it is a poor phallic symbol. I cannot imagine the female preferring a cold sharp blade of dagger piercing the "cup" of her vagina rather than the rounded tip of a warmly oiled wand.

the highest of the four qabalistic worlds; how it is the letter *J* (Yod ') in the Great Name, *Yod Heh Vav Heh,* ה ו ה '; that it represents the fundamental and purest essence of the human soul—the life force[26] itself. It is the spinal cord in the physical body, and the column of chakras in the psychic body. The wand is the Appian Way of consciousness that runs from *God*head to *your*head.

The wand is all things active, all things positive, all things protrusive and penetrating. The wand is the instrument of fatherhood, the phallus of creation, and the photons of sunlight. The wand is the hollow fennel stalk with which Prometheus brought the gift of fire (stolen from the gods) to humankind. The wand is firm; it is straight; it is singular. It is the undeviating Will of God—and ultimately, the Will of God must be the Will of the Magician.

The wand is nothing less than the pure, one-pointed purpose for which you have incarnated, and it is also the tool by which you must dispatch that sacred duty. If you think you don't have a sacred duty in life, you are profoundly mistaken. No matter what your life circumstances are, there is a job that must be done, a need that must be filled, a role that must be played in the grand comedy/drama of existence that can only be done/filled/acted out by *you and you alone.* You can be certain of this, because you wouldn't even be sitting here sucking and blowing air in and out of your lungs if there wasn't something vitally important still left undone in the universe—something that only you can do.

So why *have you* incarnated? What is your reason for existing? What is your wand? How are you using it to execute your sacred duty?

You probably don't have a good answer. Don't worry. Finding out the answer is called the "Great Work," but because you are a magician, you are actually obligated to do the Great Work. You can't let a little temporary amnesia stop you from getting on with your magical work. *You have to start somewhere,* so until you get a handle on what is your true will, just go ahead and start *pretending.* Wrap your fingers around the nearest stick and for the time being use it as your homemade wand.

---

26. The chiah.

Any pointy thing will work at first: a twig, a walking stick, a golf club, a pencil or pen (a pen is a magick wand that has changed many a world!). I cut my first wand from an almond tree in the backyard of my initiators, Phyllis and Grady McMurtry. Years later, I would, with the help of a dear brother, cut a hazel wand from Boleskine House near Loch Ness, Scotland.

Many of the traditions of ceremonial magick, especially those based on the mythology of the Hebrew Qabalah, are drawn from the Bible; and there is perhaps no Bible story more magical or dramatic than that of Moses and his miracle-working *staff.*[27]

We first see the famous staff in action when Moses, in an attempt to impress the pharaoh and his team of crack magicians, tosses his rod upon the ground and *lo and behold* it miraculously turns into a slithery snake. Not to be outdone, the pharaoh's magicians whip out their wands and throw them down, and their rods turn into snakes. But then, even as the pharaoh's magicians are high-fiving each other, Moses's snake chases down the Egyptian snakes and one by one swallows them up. After that, Moses's snake lets out a big biblical burp, straightens itself out, and stiffens back into a walking stick with a really cool handle.

The pharaoh was fascinated by this bit of Freudian one-upmanship, but not impressed enough to let the Hebrews go. Moses would have to wag his wand a few more times to finally prove to the pharaoh whose magick was bigger. With it, Moses would turn the Nile to blood and bring other deadly plagues down upon Egypt. Most memorably, the wand would save the fleeing Children of Israel from the pursuing Egyptian army when Moses created an escape route through the Red Sea by waving his magick wand over the water while shouting (in his most dramatic Charlton Heston voice), "Behold, His mighty hand!"

Moses's *hand of God* was quite a baton, and according to both magical and biblical[28] traditions, his wand was made of *almond wood*. Modern qabalistic magicians are quick to point out that the words "rod of almond" in Hebrew (מטה ה שקד) enumerate to 463. The three Hebrew

---

27. Actually, Moses's staff belonged to his brother-in-law Aaron, but nobody seems to care who had the sales receipt, because Moses ended up getting most of the press.

28. Numbers 17: 2–3 give one example.

letters that also enumerate to 463 are Tav, Samekh, and Gimel (גסת), which are associated with the three paths that form the spine (the Middle Pillar) on the Tree of Life. The Middle Pillar connects the gross matter of sephirah number ten (Malkuth) to the Supreme Consciousness of sephirah number one (Kether), the crown of absolute Godhead.

The pontifical staffs of Roman Catholic Popes have traditionally been almond rods.[29]

As a young magician, I naturally wanted an almond wand of my very own. I've described in painful detail in an earlier publication[30] the tragic adventure of my first almond wand. For the reader who is unfamiliar with the story, I will simply say that, after cutting the perfect wand from a blossoming branch of an almond tree in the Eden-esque garden of my magick teacher, Phyllis Seckler McMurtry, in Dublin, California—and after straightening it for months on a homemade straightening device—and after creating (and then executing) a two-week consecration ritual that involved invoking (as best I knew how) the spirits of fire into the wand (a ceremony that culminated on the last night with a most dramatic neighborhood calamity requiring the emergency services of the Costa Mesa Fire Department)—I then (on the very first morning I was to use it in ritual) accidentally and unceremoniously *sat* on my precious consecrated almond wand, snapping it cleanly in two.

Luckily I had another "practice" almond wand that I had surreptitiously cut in a midnight wand raid of a backyard in Huntington Beach months earlier. This time, however, instead of repeating the entire exhausting two-week consecration ceremony, I simply transferred the magical charge from the broken wand into the "new" wand by solemnly burning the

---

29. Recall the famous rod-flowering scene at the climax of Wagner's *Tannhäuser und der Sängerkrieg auf Wartburg,* where the Pope's staff miraculously blossoms to redeem the knight-singer-songwriter (which itself is reminiscent of the biblical scene in which the almond rod of the Tribe of Levi blossomed to announce God's Will that the Levites be the priestly caste of the Children of Israel).

30. Lon Milo DuQuette, *My Life with the Spirits* (Boston, MA: Weiser Books, 1999), p. 79.

pieces of the broken wand in a thurible while I rotated the new wand in the flames and repeatedly shouted, "Get in there, goddammit!"

It must have worked, because my "practice wand" continues to serve me well to this day.

While almond wood is the preferred material for qabalistic ceremonial magicians, other cultures and traditions use other woods. European Pagan traditions also abound with magick wands and staffs, and the wood most associated with the magick of Witchcraft is hazel, a fact I discovered quite accidentally in 1967 while thumbing through a very cheap occult dictionary with my songwriting partner, Charles D. Harris, as we were looking for inspiration for new songs. Our divinatory technique was simple enough. We would get out our guitars and smoke a joint of very weak commercial-grade (for 1967) Mexican marijuana, then one of us would grab the dictionary, close our eyes, and pick a page at random. We'd write a song about whatever our finger landed on … such as a *hazel wand:*

I have traveled very far
To sit here at your feet.
To ask your favor
And to make my life complete.
Touch me with your hazel wand.
Fill my heart with joy.
Bring me from darkness into light.

The naive lyrics of that refrain still blow my mind after all these years. How could we have known it was the perfect invocation, the perfect prayer? The *magick* of the hazel wand certainly worked for Charley and me (at least for two or three years), because just a couple months after we penned that song, a producer from Columbia Records heard us sing it and signed us to a record contract (Epic Records). He named the company that would publish our two singles and album[31] "Hazelwand Publishing."

---

31. Charley D. & Milo, Epic Records, "Back Bay Blu" / "The Hour Before the Dawn," 1968; "The Word Is Love" / "Annie Moon," 1969; and *Charley D. & Milo* (album), 1970.

It took me thirty-seven years, but I finally got a first-class magical hazel wand of my own. Last year, I accompanied some dear friends to Boleskine House, overlooking Loch Ness near Inverness, Scotland. At the turn of the twentieth century, it was the home of Aleister Crowley and is arguably one of the most legendary magical residences in the world. The grounds are clearly marked "Private Property" and are protected (from sophomoric Crowley fans like myself) by fencing and, if the signs are to be believed, dogs. With the help of my friends, I hopped the fence and made it close enough to the lovely house to snap a few pictures. We also brought home some hazel wands that we unceremoniously filched from the property.

Your Magick Wand

Let's now get down to specifics about how you might go about creating your magick wand.

- **Material:** As already noted, there are venerable traditions that suggest using almond or hazel wood cut in the springtime at the moment the branch is blossoming. If that is not possible, seize the opportunity whenever it presents itself. In any case, wood is universally preferred. Wands made of stone, crystal, metal, plastic, clay, paper mache or bone resonate more with the element of earth or otherwise point to other planetary associations.

- **Dimensions:** Spiritually speaking, your wand needs to be long enough to reach up to the highest heaven and down to the lowest hell. Obviously, a stick that long is hard to come by, so you should probably settle for a wand that is the approximate length of the area between the tips of your fingers and your elbow, and about as thick and round as your little finger or ring finger. It should be as straight as you can make it (more about this shortly).

- **Method of Harvesting:** If possible, you should cut your wand from the tree with a single blow. The knife, ax, or hatchet itself should have some magical significance to you. If possible, the cutting should take place on an auspicious date (your birthday, for example) or a date sacred to your own personal mythology. When you are 120 years old, you will want to be able to tell your biographer: "Why, I remember the moment I cut my magick wand. It was dawn on Easter Sunday (or noon on April Fool's Day, or sunset on the Vernal Equinox, or whatever)."

- **Preparation:**

  - **Straightening:** After you have selected and cut your wand, you will want to make it as straight as possible. This is easily done by creating a straightening jig (with a board and a few nails) and letting your wand straighten and "cure" for about sixty days.

  - **Stripping:** After your wand has been straightened, strip off the excess bark (as much as possible by hand), then sand the rough areas, knots, and tips until it is as smooth as possible. Be conscious of the natural patterns and colors of the wood, keeping an eye on the flame-like colors and designs that develop as you sand your wand smooth. This is an opportunity to get to know your wand and, in truth, is an important part of the magical "charge" with which you are imbuing it.

  - **Painting:** If you wish, you may paint your wand. It is entirely up to you. Personally, I think it looks a bit cheesy, and the natural color of the wood projects an elegance and a dignity that can only be diminished by the application of paint.

  - **Sealing:** Once you've sanded your wand smooth, you may wish to apply a clear sealer surface with a commercially available sealer, shellac, or lacquer. Personally, I don't recommend coating your wand with anything other than a natural oil, such as a good olive oil, or the magician's oil of Abramelin, or other anointing oil you might prefer. (After years of smelling magical oils growing old and rancid, I am totally turned off by so-called magical oils and perfumes. I currently use good olive oil and very little of it.)

Ideas for an On-the-Road, Improvised Homemade Wand

Here are a few things I've used on the road for my magick wand:

- A cocktail swizzle stick
- A wooden or plastic coffee stirrer
- A pencil or pen
- A chopstick
- A toothbrush

TEN

Homemade Consecration Ritual

Be this consecrated Spear
A thing of cheer, a thing of fear!
Cheer to me who wield it! —
My heart, its vigour shield it!
Fear to them who face it —
Their force, let fear disgrace it! {121}
Be a ray from the Most High,
A glance of His unsleeping eye!
That shall be fought this dreadful day!
"CONSECRATION OF THE SPEAR"
FROM *AN EVOCATION OF BARTZABEL THE SPIRIT OF MARS*[32]

---

32. *The Equinox,* vol. 1, no. 9, edited by Soror Virakam (1913; Reprint, York Beach, ME: Weiser Books, 1992), p. 117.

I hope you are beginning to see what these magical weapons really are. Any pointy thing can be a wand, and any container can be a cup, but if the pointy thing has no meaning, no connection to your will; if the container has no meaning, no connection to your capacity to love and be loved; if the sword has no meaning or connection to your mind, your wit, your imagination; if the disk has no meaning or connection to your body, your material life, your ability to function in this world; then there is no magick in any of these objects.

Once you've constructed, purchased, or otherwise obtained your magical weapons, the final step is to magically charge and dedicate them to the service of your Great Work. This is done with a consecration ceremony—sort of a graduation ceremony for magical tools. But no matter how formal or informal your ceremony is, it will be worthless, ineffective, and a complete waste of time if it doesn't actually mean something to you—unless it is uniquely your own—unless it is homemade.

The consecration ceremony can be as simple as holding the weapon in your hand and announcing to the cosmos, "This is my disk (sword, cup, wand)! I hope it works!" or as elaborate as a highly structured qabalistic ritual complete with purifications, banishings, and multiple invocations of archangels, angels, spirits, and elementals.

Your sincerity in the matter is the key to the success of the operation. Crowley and the magicians of the Golden Dawn point to what they call the "formula of the Neophyte" as the format for a proper consecration ritual. The magician simply treats the object being consecrated as if it were the candidate in an initiation ritual.

The landmarks of such a ritual are as follows:

- **The candidate is blindfolded and kept outside the temple in the outer darkness.**
  - Until the hour you have set aside for the consecration ritual, keep the object to be consecrated wrapped in a black cloth or bag.

- **The candidate is brought into the temple.**
  - For most of my magical life, my temple has been my bedroom or (when the family is out) my living room. For general

workings, the temple is a circle (real or imagined) demarcated by the four quarters. For elemental workings, such as
the consecration of magical tools, the south is associated
with fire and the wand; the west is associated with water and
the cup; the east is associated with air and the sword; and the
north is associated with earth and the disk or pantacle.

- **The candidate is examined, interrogated, allowed to pass, or, if
  for any reason found unprepared, temporarily turned away.**

  - Carefully inspect the object to be consecrated one last time
    to make sure it's finished and ready for use. If you are still
    dissatisfied in any way with the appearance of your tool,
    now is the time to make those final touch-ups.

- **The candidate is cleansed and purified (at least once) with
  water.**

  - Thoroughly clean the object to be consecrated and sprinkle
    it (even the cup) with pure water.

- **The candidate takes an oath to remain loyal to the organization
  and to abide by its regulations.**

  - Because the object to be consecrated can't actually take such
    an oath, you'll need to compose a "charge" detailing in your
    own words exactly what you expect from the tool. Spend
    some time carefully composing this charge, because if you
    are unclear in your own mind what the purpose of your
    magical tool actually is, it will be of little or no use to you.

- **The candidate is dedicated to the Great Work by a divine
  invocation.**

  - This invocation can be as brief or as elaborate as you see fit.
    At the very least, you must make some kind of symbolic ges-
    ture or prayer invoking the presence and the benediction of
    the highest divine power you are capable of imagining (even
    if you consider the highest divine power to be yourself).

- After the invocation, you might want to evoke the appropriate elemental spirits: salamanders for the wand, undines for
the cup, sylphs for the sword, and gnomes for the pantacle.
There are many wonderful and inspiring classical examples
of such operations in magical literature. One of my favorites
is Eliphas Levi's "Prayers to the Elementals."[33] The full text is
given at the end of this book.

- **The candidate is given a magical name, anointed, and robed,
then takes his or her place among the initiates.**

  - If you so choose, you may select a name for each of your
  magick weapons. The consecration ceremony is the most
  appropriate time to formally bestow that name. At the very
  least, you should seal the ceremony by anointing the weapon
  with sacred oil (olive oil if you have nothing else), and then
  place it in a new bag: a red bag for the wand, a blue or silver
  bag for the cup, a yellow bag for the sword, and a green bag
  for the disk.

Note: Even if you end up purchasing your wand, cup, sword, or disk, I
strongly advise that you sew the storage bags yourself. Anyone—even I—
can buy and cut a rectangular piece of colored cloth, fold it in half, and
hand-sew two sides with colored thread. The minutes you spend doing
this are priceless magical moments that will be stored in your magical
memory, forever linking to your weapons and the powers they embody.

Use your magical tools often—for your daily rituals and anytime you
arrange your altar. Keep them constantly in the forefront of your consciousness. Regularly take them out of their bags and oil, polish, and clean
them. Even these simple acts of maintenance are magical meditations of
the highest order. Care for your wand, cup, sword, and disk as you would
your most sacred and priceless treasures in the universe, for that is exactly
what they are.

And please, try to not accidentally sit on them!

---

33. Found in Eliphas Levi's *Dogme et Rituel de la Haute Magie* [Transcendental
Magic: Its Doctrine and Ritual], 1854–1856. Translator unknown.

Postscript to Magical Weapons

—OR—
IF YOU CAN'T MAKE MAGICK OUT OF PAPER MACHE, YOU WON'T BE ABLE TO MAKE MAGICK OUT OF GOLD

Reading the ancient grimoires, one might assume that the magicians of old were already wealthy and independent individuals able to dedicate entire rooms of their house to performing magick; able to buy or fabricate golden talismans, crowns, rings, and medallions; able to build elaborate altars, chests, and magical cabinets; able to drink from silver chalices and brandish daggers and swords of gleaming steel; able to dress themselves in costly silk vestments sewn with threads of gold and encrusted with precious stones.

It is true that a certain amount of magical virtue resides in precious objects and possessions. You care for them. You think about them. You protect them. You maintain them meticulously. You store them carefully. You treat them with respect. It is also true that different materials are characterized by their unique molecular structure, atomic weight, and rate of nuclear decay. Gold *is* different from wood. Diamond vibrates differently than glass. Steel is more formidable than paper. Consciously and subconsciously, we respond differently to different substances and materials.

Magick is, after all, a spiritual artform. The magician is an artist, and artists must feel comfortable and confident with the tools of their work. If money is no object to you, then arming and adorning yourself with expensive and beautiful instruments and accoutrements will probably add an elegant and stylish touch to your magical work. But make no mistake: If you can't transform a scrap of paper into a magick ring, then there will be no magick power in a golden ring. If you can't transform a plastic cup into a magick cup, then there will be no magick power in a silver chalice.

The magick comes from you, not the material.

Late in the 1970s, Constance and I were studying and preparing to celebrate our first Gnostic Mass. It is an elaborate eucharistic ceremony celebrating the Grail mysteries. The celebrants are the Priest and Priestess.

The Priest bears a sacred lance, which was easy enough to make. (I painted a broom handle and topped it with a brass spear-point a friend *borrowed* from a decorative flag stand at the local American Legion Post.)

During the ceremony, the Priestess crowns the Priest with a crown that is described in detail in the text of the mass:

> *The crown may be of gold or platinum, or of electrum magicum; but with no other metals, save the small proportions necessary to a proper alloy. It may be adorned with divers jewels, at will. But it must have the Uraeus serpent twined about it … [34]*

Obviously, obtaining a crown as described was just not going to happen. So instead of going to the jeweler and commissioning a gold or platinum or electrum magicum Uraeus serpent with jeweled eyes (yeah, right!), I did the next best thing. I made my sacred Priest's crown out of paper mache.

---

34. From *Liber XV, O.T.O.*, "Ecclesiae Gnosticae Catholicae Canon Missae" by Aleister Crowley. Found in various reference works, including *The Magick of Aleister Crowley* by Lon Milo DuQuette (York Beach, ME: Weiser Books, 2003), p. 229.

I unwound a wire coat hanger and had Constance wrap it around my head until it fit (it hurt!). I twisted the hook in such a way that it was positioned above my forehead. I went into the garage and found a stack of newspapers, then scrounged around under the kitchen sink and found an old plastic dish pan. I used our paper cutter to quickly and wildly cut a few days of newspapers into strips.

Into the dish pan I dumped about a cup of Constance's whole-wheat pastry flour and a big pinch of salt. I then added what we had left of a bottle of Elmer's white glue (I suppose it was almost a half cup). I then quickly added a little more than a cup of warm tap water. I used Constance's best cooking whisk to mix it up (big mistake!) until I had a sticky paste.

I had no idea what I was doing. I just started dipping strips of newspaper in the paste and then wrapping the wire with the newspaper. After many layers, it actually began to look like something. I played with the wire as I went along and stretched pieces of paper to form the serpent's head and hood. I took a few hours, but when I finally set it out in the patio to dry, it looked like it might actually work.

The next morning I tried it on, readjusted a few things, patched a few rough spots, and more accurately formed the head and hood with paper and a little reconstituted paste. The next day I spray-painted it a brilliant metallic gold and glued two rhinestone rubies for its eyes.

Every few years I have to repaint it and touch up a few things, but my coat-hanger/paper-mache crown has served me well for over thirty-five years. To me it is more precious, more magical, than *gold or platinum, or electrum magicum.*

The magick comes from the magician, and a magician can make anything from anything. Your creative potential is endless … like that of paper mache.

Constance and I celebrating a Gnostic Mass in the living room of our home in Costa Mesa, California, c. 1985. Visible are a few examples of homemade and improvised magical tools, furniture, and accoutrements. The gold crown of the Priest is made of a coat hanger and paper mache. My lance is a painted broom handle mounted with a spear-point "borrowed" from a decorative flagstaff. The font is our living-room end table with a large seashell for the bowl and a small shell to hold the salt. The pew in the background is an antique prelate's seat donated to the lodge by a generous member. My robe was sewn in the early 1970s by Phyllis Seckler for her then husband, Grady McMurtry. He wore this robe when he initiated me into the O.T.O. in 1975.

———

Need a magical object? Make it out of paper mache! Here, Constance is blow-drying a mask of Dionysus as we prepare for another Rite of Jupiter. The magick square of Jupiter is seen just behind her.

———

PART III

A Magical Lodge in Your Home

The fire lighting ceremony from the opening of the Rite of Mars, c. 1986. Constance goes to the altar and conjures over a large bowl:

"I swear by Djinn and by Shin and by the space between that I will not stir from this place until the fire of God hath flamed upon the water that is upon the altar. Dost thou hear, Brother Ash?

"By Aub, the witchery of the secret flame; by Aud, the sublety of the inmost fluid; by Aur, the effulgence of the radiant light. I call thee, Ash! I adore thee, Ash! Ash! Ash! Ash!

"I caress thee! I kiss thee! I suck thee up into my mouth and nostrils! Ohooatan! Ohooatan! Ohooatan!" (She lights the flame.) Behold! The fire of God upon the altar as I have sworn by Djinn and by Shin and by the space between!"

Constance does this very well. In fact, she blows everyone's minds.

———

Our living room/dining room cleared and set up for our celebration of a Gnostic Mass, c. 1987.

The Gnostic Mass is the central ceremony of the O.T.O., public and private. For years, Constance and I regularly celebrated this beautiful ritual in our home for lodge members and guests.

Shown in this picture are the high altar and super altar with the required accoutrements, including a homemade Stele of Revealing in the center, twenty-two candles, roses, a cup, and a paten. Our living-room end tables serve as our fire altar (seen here with the incense and censer), and our font is the large seashell seen in the extreme foreground (along with a smaller seashell that holds salt). Not seen in this picture are the two pillars on either side of the high altar and the veil, which is closed in front of the high altar during part of the ceremony.

The congregation sat on every chair we could round up and on our antique pew, and floor cushions were arranged along the sides of the room. We could comfortably seat twenty congregants and uncomfortably accommodate thirty.

The dining room being transformed for an evening performance of a homemade Rite of Saturn, the first of the seven Rites of Eleusis, c. 1985.

Even the rehearsals for these homemade rituals become master classes in magick, mythology, and astrology. Because the Rites of Eleusis tell the mythological and astrological stories of the seven traditional planetary spheres, two officers in each rite are identified as the zodiac sign that the planet rules (or is exalted in). In this photo, Constance has just set up two chairs, borrowed from Jean-Paul's bedroom, to be the thrones for Brothers Aquarius and Capricorn (Saturn rules Aquarius and Capricorn).

Behind the veil (representing the Abyss on the qabalistic Tree of Life) is the throne of Saturn. The Saturn altar, seen between the pillars, displays the Seal of Saturn on the magick square of Saturn, and supports a human skull (real and perfectly legal) surrounded by red roses. The pillar in the center of the dining room holds a brass bowl that will be filled with alcohol and burned during the ceremony. The room is festooned with sprigs of bougainvillea, which I quietly snipped from the neighborhood.

ELEVEN

Think You Have Nowhere to Go to Learn Magick? Start Teaching What You Wish to Learn!

O.T.O.
ORDO TEMPLI ORIENTIS
CHARTER
HERU-RA-HA LODGE

**Peace, Tolerance, Truth, Salutation on All Points of the Triangle,
Respect to the Order
To All Whom It May Concern Greeting and Health
Do what thou wilt shall be the whole of the Law.
Oyez! Oyez! Oyez!
Know ye all that I, Caliph Hymenaeus Alpha,
do hereby certify, acknowledge and proclaim that our**

Brother Lon Milo DuQuette
Is authorized to establish and maintain a Lodge of O.T.O.
in the Valley of
Orange County, California,
and to accept, initiate, and instruct individuals
living in or near said Valley
subject only to agreeable regulations that may be
proposed by the Caliph.
Love is the law, love under will.
Witness my hand and seal this day, January 7, 1978, E.V.
[Signed and sealed:]
Hymenaeus Alpha[35]
Ordo Templi Orientis
Caliph

The cost of giving is receiving.[36]

During a recent radio interview I was asked the question:

"You've written sixteen books on subjects relating to ceremonial magick. Your biography says you've taught magick for thirty-five years. Just what are your 'credentials' to speak authoritatively on this unusual subject?"

It was a good question, and one that deserved a good answer. Frankly, I didn't have one. I've had no formal instruction or training in any spiritual disciplines. I hold no academic degrees. I've attended no seminary. Hell, I only graduated from *high school* because I had the lead in the school musical.

I scrambled for an on-air response, and the best I could come up with was one that sounded impressive enough at the time but was a bit misleading and not altogether accurate:

"I've just been interested in magick and the occult since my late teens, and in the 1970s I was lucky enough to come in contact with three people [Israel Regardie, Phyllis Seckler, and Grady McMurtry] who were once

---

35. Grady L. McMurtry.

36. *A Course in Miracles* (Mill Valley, CA: Foundation for Inner Peace, 1976), p. 275.

students of the great English magician Aleister Crowley. After about thirty years of just studying and practicing what I loved, I woke up one morning and realized that most of the people in the world who knew more than I about this stuff ... were now dead."

Up to a point, all that was true. I did indeed know and study with these three famous and legendary magicians. I benefitted immeasurably from their counsel and instruction. (Phyllis was actually my formal A∴A∴ superior). These magical heroes and mentors, however, did not actually teach me magick. In fact, I really didn't start to *learn* magick until I started to *teach* magick.

As I mentioned earlier, Constance and I have been active in the magical organization Ordo Templi Orientis since the mid-1970s. In January of 1978, I was authorized to charter a lodge of O.T.O., initiate individuals into the Order, and host other events such as classes, Gnostic Masses, and social activities. The character of our lodge has evolved over the years along with the growth of this remarkable (and sometimes controversial) organization.

Early on, Constance and I (by virtue of our relative seniority in the tiny, newly resurrected O.T.O.) were needed to initiate members into the lower degrees. A few years later, as other initiatory bodies began to form around the country and the world, we were needed to initiate members into the higher degrees. Eventually, more and more initiates could fulfill those functions and our focus turned to other organizational areas that needed our attention. These duties were not burdens we bore for the sake of our magical evolution. On the contrary, it was as if the universe was anticipating our every personal magical need, and our work in the Order was simply the most convenient way for us to fulfill and work out those issues on the material plane.

Obviously, there are very few people in the world who will ever find themselves in the particular position we found ourselves in, and I admit that our case was (and is) relatively unique. Nevertheless, our involvement in a highly structured magical organization does not in any way exempt us from the necessity of creating, building, and sustaining our magical world and careers from scratch out of entirely homemade elements.

Our lodge, Heru-ra-ha Lodge, O.T.O., is the oldest local body char-tered by a Grand Lodge in the Order. In the last thirty-five years, we've hosted over 1,700 classes and performed hundreds of initiations, Gnos-tic Masses, and other ceremonies (some very complex, requiring mul-tiple rooms festooned with elaborate furnishings). We've fed multitudes of hungry candidates and initiates and hosted scores of public lectures, workshops, plays, feasts, weddings, memorials, and celebrations.

All these events (sometimes as many as five a week) were held in our home—while we raised a wonderful son to manhood, and while I worked a full-time job and Constance worked part-time. For thirty-five years, our modest, rented house—our living room, our dining room, our bedroom, our garage, our backyard—has been abbey, temple, mon-astery, preceptory, cathedral, rectory, classroom, lecture hall, chapel, profess house, initiation chamber, magick space … *holy ground.*

Our furniture has always had to do double duty. End tables transform into altar and font; decorative swords, lances, and banners are pulled from the walls and wielded in sacred ceremonies; dining room tables serve as altars or are covered and adorned with blazing bowls of fire and statues and secret symbols—household items that, after the mystic ceremony is over, quietly return to their camouflaged stations as quaint household items and Grandma's curious bric-a-brac.

DuQuette magick is patently homemade. We know no other way to operate. When you enter our home (which has been described as "Beat-rix Potter meets H. P. Lovecraft"), you enter a temple—but you also en-ter a school.

In 1978, shortly after our lodge was chartered, we started a weekly magick class in our home. It was (and still is) open to anyone prepared to behave themselves in our house for a little over two hours. Class is free, though a donation basket is painfully conspicuous. Even with my travel schedule, we seldom miss a Monday Night Magick Class. We've averaged fifty classes a year for the last thirty-five years (and for three years we held class twice a week). We live for class, for we learn far more than what we teach.

In the early days, I was hard-pressed to stay one week ahead of the class in my mastery of the various magical subjects. Eventually, I gave up all pretense of acting like some kind of authority (nobody believed it anyway) and surrendered to the fact that I was learning magick as I was teaching it. By simply trying to explain things to others, I discovered that I was also explaining them for the first time to myself. I truly didn't realize how much I already *knew* until I started to teach. Perhaps more importantly, I didn't know what I *needed to learn* until I started to teach. I didn't know what I *didn't know*.

Enochian magick skrying session in the living room, c. 1979. Enochian vision magick is one of the most dramatic and effectual of all the magical systems we've practiced and taught. Often referred to as "angel magick," it was developed in the late 1500s by Dr. John Dee, the brilliant scientist and counselor to Queen Elizabeth I. The details of how the system was received have fascinated magicians, scholars, and linguists for centuries. The magician enters into an altered state of consciousness as the result of intoning (or hearing) "calls" in the Angelic language. He or she then communicates directly in vision with individual "angels" in a complex and anal-retentively organized cosmos.

In this photo, a class member sits before a large, three-dimensional elemental tablet of union, made up of twenty colored truncated pyramids that are the "homes" to the letters of the names of the four great archangels of the elements: EXARP (air), HCOMA (water), NANTA (earth), and BITOM (fire). I have just banished the living room temple with the wand, and Constance has purified the temple and the holy table with water. One class member reads the call from the book while another sits before the tablet of union and describes what he is seeing in vision.

———

So, if you think you have nowhere to go to learn magick, you're wrong. Your own home is the campus of the only true magical university you will ever attend, and you are the dean, the faculty, and the janitor.

If your life circumstances are such that you can accommodate a few guests in your living room one night a week, I strongly encourage you to at least consider offering an informal class right in your home. Don't worry if you don't think you know enough. Just schedule the class and study the very things you most wish to learn. It works like magick. Post a small, attractive, and well-worded notice at your local bookstore, college, or natural foods store. If you are concerned about giving out your address, screen your prospective students by chatting a few times back and forth via e-mail or meeting them at a coffee shop.

Schedule the class and then hold it. Even if only one person shows up, hold it. Even if no one shows up, hold it.

What are you interested in? Magick? Grab a good book on magick and use it as your text. *Modern Magick*[37] by my friend Donald Michael Kraig is a great instructional text, as is my book *The Magick of Aleister Crowley.*[38]

Interested in astrology? There are plenty of texts out there to begin with, and plenty of free online astrological calculators. Offer a class where everyone casts their own natal chart from scratch using their birth information. (Don't know how to do that? Learn how along with the class.) Then, to understand a little about the charts you cast, systematically learn

37. Donald Michael Kraig, *Modern Magick: Eleven Lessons in the High Magickal Arts* (Saint Paul, MN: Llewellyn Publications, 1988).

38. Lon Milo DuQuette, *The Magick of Aleister Crowley: A Handbook of the Rituals of Thelema* (York Beach, ME: Weiser Books, 2003). First published as *The Magick of Thelema* in 1993.

about the planets, zodiac signs, and aspects as they appear in each of your charts.

Interested in Tarot? Lots of people are. Put up a flyer at a health food store and your living room will be packed. Get a deck of Tarot cards and a good text by Mary Greer[39] or Rachel Pollack,[40] or even my Tarot of Ceremonial Magick[41] (and book by the same name[42]) or Crowley's master text *The Book of Thoth*.[43] Spend a few weeks on the trumps. Learn which cards represent planets and elements and signs of the zodiac. Then spend a few weeks on the small cards, and by doing so learn the basics of Qabalah without even trying.

Just schedule the time and host the class. *The class itself is the magick.* The subject matter is secondary to the fact that you and your guests are magicians meeting to discuss, practice, and live magick. Help each other. Soon your weekly gatherings will take on a life of their own; strangers become friends, friends become colleagues, and colleagues become an informal homemade magical order.

You can conduct your classes however you see fit, but we'd like to share a few secrets that we believe have helped our Monday Night Magick Class endure and thrive for thirty-five years.

- Have a consistent and regular schedule. In the long run, more people will attend more often and consistently if the class is held *every week* rather than biweekly or monthly. Classes should not be shorter than ninety minutes or longer than two hours. Special workshops can be longer.

---

39. Mary K. Greer, *Mary K. Greer's 21 Ways to Read a Tarot Card* (Woodbury, MN: Llewellyn Publications, 2006).

40. Rachel Pollack, *Rachel Pollack's Tarot Wisdom: Spiritual Teachings and Deeper Meanings* (Woodbury, MN: Llewellyn Publications, 2008).

41. Lon Milo DuQuette, *Tarot of Ceremonial Magick* (deck), *Babalon Edition* (Washington, DC: Thelesis Aura, 2010).

42. Lon Milo DuQuette, *Tarot of Ceremonial Magick* (York Beach, ME: Weiser Books, 1995).

43. Aleister Crowley, *The Book of Thoth: A Short Essay on the Tarot of the Egyptians* (London: O.T.O., 1944); *The Equinox*, vol. 3, no. 5 (Reprint, York Beach, ME: Samuel Weiser, 1992).

- With all due respects to the free-spirited traditions we might have held dear in our inconsiderate and unsophisticated youth, "Pagan Standard Time" is for amateurs. Start on time (within fifteen minutes) and end on time!

- Conduct each class as if there were both complete novices and experienced magicians in attendance (there will be anyway!). In your comments, endeavor to put everything in basic, fundamental terms the neophyte can grasp, and at the same time give the adept something new and provocative to think about. The adepts will appreciate the review, and the newcomers will get a glimpse of what is to come.

- Don't even dream about making class a money-making enterprise! Don't charge money for class. Don't even suggest a set donation amount. Five dollars will be too much for a member who *can't* afford it, and a hundred dollars won't be enough for a member who *can* afford it. Point out the donation basket at the beginning and end of class and then take your chances that you'll get enough to pay for the tea and handouts.

- Your house should be clean, vacuumed and uncluttered. If you can't clean your house for class, you can't banish a demon from your temple. It's the least you can do for your students. In fact, for some people, the sight of a clean, organized, and attractive magician's home will be evidence that you are in possession of supernatural powers the likes of which they have never before beheld.

- Provide tea at the beginning of class, but do not encourage food or snacks. Snacks, except on very special occasions, can take up half the class if you let them, and have you cleaning up the kitchen until midnight.

- Engage the class. If you are reading from a text, pass the book around (or print out copies) and let each member read a few sentences or paragraphs. Round-robin reading is fun and it keeps everyone awake and focused on the material. Each week, ask for a class member to volunteer to have a dictionary at hand to look up unfamiliar words that inevitably appear in magical literature.

- If you are doing rituals, let as many class members as possible participate.

- Do magick...just don't talk about it. Make talismans, magick tools, and robes. Learn about these things as you make them. Group rituals, skrying sessions, chanting, even silent meditations take you from theory and thrust you into practice.

- Allow, even encourage, short bursts of silliness. Allow running gags to develop. Reward class members who make comments that are particularly brilliant or funny by tossing them foreign coins or some other kind of worthless treasure. Prepare home-made diplomas and certificates for long-running class series. Above all, have fun!

- Allow member interest to guide your choice of class subject, *but class should not be a democracy!* (No one but you, however, should be aware of that fact.)

Finally, I'll end this chapter with a couple of "thou shalt nots":

- Thou shalt not be a megalomaniac. Nobody knows everything about magick and the occult, so don't act like you know everything or that you even know much more than your students. Be prepared to say "I don't know" a lot! Be prepared to say, "I stand corrected." Rejoice in your students knowing more than you, because that means you've done well.

- Thou shalt never say, "That is a question beyond your grade level." In other words, thou shalt not be degree-exclusive. The best class is open to everyone who is willing to behave in your house for two hours. Even if there are class members who belong to a particular coven or a certain magical order, *while they are in your house and at your class, everyone is equal, members and non-members alike.* Don't be a snob! With the exception of the secret words, handshakes, and signs of recognition, there is nothing secret in even the most secret societies. If someone asks you an advanced, esoteric question, *answer it* in the clearest way you can. If you don't know the answer, say, "Good question! I don't know!"

- Finally, *thou shalt not hit upon thy class members!* If you need to troll for lovers, do it somewhere other than in your class. There is nothing more despicable than a person in a perceived position of authority who attempts to use his or her position to seduce a student. It is unethical and evidence of a flawed character—and if there is one thing we should all avoid in the world of magick, it is hanging out with flawed characters.

Good luck!

TWELVE

Raising Children in a Magical Home

Your children are not your children.
They are the sons and daughters of Life's longing for itself.
They come through you but not from you,
And though they are with you yet they belong not to you.
KAHLIL GIBRAN[44]

Children—all children—are magical beings. When a child is present, you are in the presence of a god. That little kid is the most powerful, awesome, and terrible magician in the room, and you will surely suffer if you don't pay close attention. The child will soon enough grow into a floundering grownup like yourself, but for a few golden years you have the opportunity to learn from a master.

This doesn't mean that you must put your magick on hold in order to raise a child. On the contrary, the moment the baby is born, your life

---

44. Kahlil Gibran, *The Prophet* (New York: Alfred A. Knopf, 1923), p. 17.

gets really magical. But as a parent/magician, you must be perpetually mindful of the fact that the child is an ever-present and integral factor in the equation of your magical life. Try as you might, you cannot avoid the implications of this immutable fact of life.

In the spring of 1971, Constance and I had been married for nearly four years. One afternoon we both were struck with the same irrational conviction that it was time for us to have a baby. We did some quick calculating in our heads and determined that if conception happened immediately, the baby would be born on Constance's birthday, February 27. Eschewing our usual contraceptive precautions (and ignoring the afternoon sun), we joyously (and with full intent) proceeded to conceive a child. It was no trouble at all.

About a month later, while attending church services at the Self-Realization Fellowship temple in Fullerton, Constance fainted (it was more like an ecstatic swoon) and I had to help her outside to the temple gardens. There, sitting on a marble bench in the cool, shaded garden, she blissfully announced that she was now sure she was pregnant. She was right, and on February 27, 1972, we woke up and said, "Today's the day we're having the baby!"

We took a long walk to El Matador (our favorite Mexican restaurant) and gorged on guacamole, chips, and cheese. Then, as if we were not stuffed enough, we walked even farther away from home to Thrifty Drug Store for a double-scoop ice cream cone.

We waddled home from our gluttonous adventure in the late afternoon and amused ourselves by playing penny ante poker, and mused over the fact that we still hadn't chosen a name for the baby. Early in the evening, Constance's water broke and we were off to the hospital in my light-green 1950 Chrysler Windsor (which we named Martha).

Constance brought along a framed picture of our favorite guru at the time, Paramahansa Yogananda, which she set up at her bedside in the labor room. His serene image comforted us both immensely during that long night. Our beautiful baby boy was born a little over six hours later than we had calculated nine months earlier, and our lives instantly became even more profoundly magical.

Several days later, we settled on the name, Jean-Paul. On our first date back in high school, Constance had told me she wanted six children. She had names for all of them. The first was to be named "Jean-Paul." I was really hoping she would forget the other five children idea.

Even though for the next twenty years we would be operating a very active magical lodge out of our house, we tried to raise our son in the most "normal" environment possible. It was as if the three of us were growing up together. We never excluded him from lodge activities (with the exception of the super-secret O.T.O. initiation ceremonies), and we took him with us everywhere. Lodge and class members became our extended family and provided him with a collection of colorful aunts and uncles whose love continues to bless our lives.

For his part, Jean-Paul was always a very good sport, sharing his home and his parents with countless out-of-town guests, taking part in rites and plays (for years he read the parts of all the fairies in our backyard performances of *A Midsummer Night's Dream*), and helping move furniture to prepare for masses and initiations. The three of us were a team. We amused ourselves, and we amused each other. We were and still are our own best audience and best friends. We opened our home to Jean-Paul's school friends, who also enjoyed the colorful craziness of the eccentric DuQuette household. We remain friends with all of them.

Jupiter, c. 1982. Our son grew up amid a heavy schedule of magical events, public and private. Several of the seven planetary Rites of Eleusis afford rich opportunities for children to dress up and be part of the fun.

This photo is from the Rite of Jupiter. In mythology, Jupiter (or Zeus) is the jovial and beneficent father god. He is also the father of Dionysus, god of wine and ecstasy, and so the Rite of Jupiter is intended to be lots of fun for all involved. The costuming and decorations follow a strict color scheme dictated by the particular planetary sphere on the qabalistic Tree of Life each rite concerns itself with. The sphere of Jupiter (Chesed), being number four on the Tree of Life, is dominated by blues and purples. The costumes include accessories sacred to Zeus (such as eagles and thunderbolts) and Dionysus (such as snakes, leopard skins, and grapes). Here we see the boys wearing ivy wreaths, leopard skin (faux), grapes, and rubber snakes.

———

Magick is not a "belief system" as the term is commonly understood, so there was really not much *doctrine* with which we could *indoctrinate* Jean-Paul. Therefore, there was little for him to rebel against. Besides instructing him to always use common sense and logic when evaluating spiritual or philosophical ideas, we encouraged him to develop his own spiritual worldview. We exposed him to a broad spectrum of religious ideas and never pressured him to *believe* anything. As far as I can determine, our lifestyle provided a safe, nurturing, stimulating, and (for as wild and crazy as things were) *wholesome* environment for a child to grow up in. We couldn't be prouder of the man he has become.

Constance and I are both of the opinion (although there is no way to prove this) that the child chooses the parents, and does so for reasons that none of us can or ever will completely understand with our meat brains. We may have our personal opinions and theories of child rearing, but neither of us would ever dream of telling another parent how to raise their child. That being said, I have a few suggestions that might be helpful for magicians with children.

- Don't make a big, spooky, dramatic deal about your magical studies and practices. Your involvement in magick might be dark, spooky, and mysterious to your parents and grandparents, but it shouldn't be a dark or spooky thing for your children. It should be intelligent, fun, logical, beautiful, and, above all, *normal*. To that end...

- Don't behave as if the rest of the world is persecuting you for your magical beliefs or lifestyle.

- Don't suggest that your involvement in magick is in any way dangerous, sinful, or illegal.

- Don't expect children to understand the metaphoric "reality" of angels, demons, and gods.

- Set a positive example. If the practice of magick makes you happy, let your children see and share in your happiness. If the practice of magick does not make you happy ... get into something else!

Parenting is, always has been, and always shall be a challenging and sometimes frustrating endeavor. Your parents weren't perfect, and you won't be perfect either. Be prepared to forgive your parents for their imperfections, and if you're lucky, your own children will someday forgive you for yours. Your magick will not help you if you cannot free yourself of both the past *and* the future.

THIRTEEN

Magick on the Road

All journeys have secret destinations of which the traveler is unaware.

MARTIN BUBER

Being an initiating officer in the O.T.O. has over the years afforded me the opportunity to travel worldwide quite a bit on Order business, and my subsequent writing and musical careers have more recently added other events to my travel itinerary. I like to travel, and I am for the most part a good traveler. I enjoy the disciple and focus travel demands of me. I enjoy the solitude of the journey. I enjoy the long hours of quiet self-sufficiency when I'm alone with my thoughts. I delight in a perpetual background meditation of not knowing exactly what adventures await me along the way and at my destination.

Each trip is a complex magical "ceremony" within which are multiple smaller ceremonies all needing artful coordination and precise timing. Funding must be invoked. Scheduling obstacles must be banished. Spirits (manager, airlines, friends, colleagues, bookstore managers, club owners, guitar rental stores, cab drivers, hotel reservation and desk clerks, etc.) must be conjured and charged (appeased, cajoled, directed, and compensated)—

all this even before I am ready to focus on the main object of the operation (the initiation, business meeting, lecture, workshop, seminar, book signing, recording session, concert, etc.).

Of course, you could say that I'm simply applying fancy magical terminology to mundane events, and you would be correct. But for a magician, there are no mundane events. I meant every word of what I wrote in chapter 0: "... once you realize you are a magician, it will be impossible for you to remove the magick from any aspect of your existence." It's all magick, and every moment of your existence you are called upon to be a magician. Airport delays, waiting at the gate, and tedious hours in the air offer me opportunities to practice *pranayama* and mentally banish, invoke, or silently chant my magical mantra. Even standing in slow-moving lines and passing through the dreadful security procedures at airports can be transformed into an initiation ceremony that echoes with uncanny similarities the *passing of the pylons* of the Egyptian *Book of the Dead*, if only one has magical eyes to see it as such.

But there are also occasions while traveling when I unexpectedly find it necessary to perform a more formal impromptu or "emergency" magical operation using improvised magical accoutrements and weapons. I can think of no clearer example of homemade magick in action than these rituals that I have had to throw together in hotel rooms, public lavatories, or even the backseats of taxi cabs. Here are just a couple of examples of how I operate *in the field*, so to speak.

Traveling as much as I do each year, I'm used to quickly setting up housekeeping in hotel rooms and living out of my suitcase. Obviously I don't travel around the world with all my magical furnishings and tools. I don't bring my elemental banners or symbolic decorations that festoon the working area of my home temple, nor do I bring along my magical robes or my wand, cup, sword, and disk. I've never traveled with the heavy and elaborate furniture (holy table and elemental tablets) that I use to perform Enochian vision magick, and when I'm required to summon spirits and demons in Goetic/Solomonic operations, I certainly don't pull out of my suitcase a magic circle (nine feet in diameter) and a triangle and placards of divine names.

I do, however, always travel with a deck of Tarot cards, and the cards (together with a few common items I can scavenge from the hotel) are usually all I need to construct a viable magick temple anywhere and execute a first-rate magical ceremony.

A deck of Tarot cards is a magick temple (indeed, an entire universe) in a box. Each card represents a particular facet of the magical universe around us and within us. The deck is the ultimate pantacle—organized upon the purest of qabalistic principles. There is no aspect of consciousness that cannot be located *on* or represented *by* one or more Tarot cards. Even "nothingness" can be found in the formless inscrutability of the Tarot. In fact, everything I have ever needed to build a homemade temple while away from home, I have conveniently found in a deck of Tarot cards. Here's a quick example of how it's done.

Hotel-Room Homemade Temple

After performing my customary banishing ritual (most usually a version of the pentagram ritual), I create the perimeter of my temple space by acknowledging and marking the sacred quarters in the cardinal directions. Of course I do this in my mind, but in order to ground my understanding of where in the cosmos I am, I place the four aces of the Tarot in the quarters of the room as unmistakable emblems of the elements and the magick they embody.

There are two distinctly different ways the four aces can be assigned to the quarters, depending on whether the temple is to be arranged for microcosmic or macrocosmic workings.

Elemental Temple (Microcosmic)

For rituals based on the elements (fire, water, air, earth, and spirit), I create a "microcosmic" temple. I imagine myself standing on the surface of the earth with the four quarters assigned according to the classic elemental rulerships of the four terrestrial winds: Ace of Swords (air) in the east, Ace of Wands (fire) in the south, Ace of Cups (water) in the west, and Ace of Disks (earth) in the north.

Planetary/Zodiacal Temple (Macrocosmic)

For planetary or zodiacal (macrocosmic) workings, I project myself into a much larger universe, and imagine myself positioned as the sun surrounded by the belt of the zodiac. In this greater universe, the four quarters are assigned according to where the cardinal zodiac signs (one each for fire, water, air, and earth) are positioned: Ace of Wands (cardinal fire, Aries) in the east; Ace of Disks (cardinal earth, Capricorn) in the south; Ace of Swords (cardinal air, Libra) in the west; and the Ace of Cups (cardinal water, Cancer) in the north.

Note: For Enochian magick rituals, the four aces of the Tarot are also representative of the archangelic and angelic powers and personages of the four elemental tablets. In my deck, the Tarot of Ceremonial Magick,[45] the full image of each Enochian elemental tablet is actually displayed on the appropriate ace. The use of these cards as the four "walls" of your magick temple, along with the proper rituals to charge them, is a most effective way to ceremonially create sacred space in which to perform magick operations or meditations.

Very often the placing of the aces in the four quarters is all that is necessary to create the sacred space I need. But for more elaborate workings, I also cast a homemade magick *circle* in the center of the sacred space.

Hotel-Room Homemade Magick Circle

For ceremonies of spirit evocation (Goetia, or Solomonic magick as presented in traditional texts such as the first book of the *Lemegeton: The Lesser Key of Solomon*),[46] the magician stands within a protective circle

---

45. Lon Milo DuQuette, *Tarot of Ceremonial Magick* (deck), *Babalon Edition* (Washington, DC: Thelesis Aura, 2010).

46. *The Book of the Goetia of Solomon the King: Translated into the English Tongue by a Dead Hand and Adorned with Divers Other Matters Germane Delightful to the Wise: The Whole Edited, Verified, Introduced and Commented by Aleister Crowley*. Most recent edition, with engraved illustrations of the spirits, by M. L. Breton and foreword by Hymenaeus Beta (York Beach, ME: Samuel Weiser, 1996). Known as the *Lesser Key of Solomon*, it is the first book of the *Lemegeton* (c. 1687). Translated by S. L. MacGregor Mathers, the "Dead Hand" referred to in the full title above. From the Sloane manuscripts nos. 2731 and 3648 found in the British Library.

surrounded by a litany of divine names. Placed outside circle is the triangle, also surrounded by magick words of power. The triangle (theoretically) traps the spirit or demon that has been summoned by the magician's prayers and conjurations, and constrains it long enough for it to receive its instructions from the magician. For years, when doing this kind of magick, I took a lot of time and expended a great amount of energy (pushing my artistic skills to their limits) to create the classic circle and triangle as described in the traditional texts. As the years passed, I eventually became comfortable with my understanding of what was actually going on inside my psyche during operations of this nature. As a consequence, I have dramatically simplified my operating procedures, streamlined my circle and triangle, and abandoned much of the elaborate trappings and medieval (and superstition-inspired) choreography that filled the ancient books. Today, my Goetic magick circle is simply a thin silk cord that I can wrap up and put in my pocket (or, when necessary, wrap around my body so I can "stay in the circle" for extended periods of time), and my triangle is a segmented carpenter's ruler.

But the magick circle is (or should be) more than just a magical prophylactic that we roll on before we penetrate the infernal realms of Goetic demons. For countless practices, the casting of the circle (and understanding what you are doing when you cast the circle) is, in and of itself, a magical ceremony of the highest order. The aces in the quarters establish the *holy ground* of our temple, but the circle is the *Holy of Holies*, where we elevate and unite our consciousness with that of the Supreme Consciousness, and where we stand to banish or invoke elements, planets, and gods. It is the *sacred space* in which we sit or lie down to induce visions; it the *high place* from which we call forth angels; it is the *sanctuary* where we can safely leave our physical bodies during out-of-body experiences. The circle is our *workroom* where we consecrate talismans and magical weapons; it is our *monk's cell*, our *meditation chamber*, our *alchemical laboratory*, our *wedding chamber*, or, simply, a quiet place to worship and adore the Supreme Consciousness of the cosmos.

Tarot Cards Again to the Rescue

I use Tarot cards to create a beautiful and powerful homemade magick circle that I can construct anywhere in just a few minutes. Briefly, here's how it works.

For macrocosmic workings, the circle can be viewed as the belt of the zodiac, with you, the magician, as the sun at the center. Right off the bat, this is a very cool meditation!

The cards we use to form the circle are the thirty-six *small cards* of the Tarot (the 2, 3, 4, 5, 6, 7, 8, 9, and 10 of each of the four suits).

Note: You might think there are forty small cards (the ace through 10 of each suit), but technically the aces are *not* small cards. The aces are actually the master cards of their suits—the 2 through 10s of the suits live inside their aces. Are you following me so far? Good.

The thirty-six small cards represent the thirty-six *decans* (or periods of ten degrees) of the zodiac, and the zodiacal year. When laid out in a counterclockwise ring, these thirty-six cards will form our magick circle. The small card/decans pass through the zodiacal year from Aries all the way through Pisces in a most elegant and logical manner.

Recall that the suit of wands represents (among many other things) the element of fire, the suit of cups represents water, the suit of swords represents air, and the suit of disks represents earth.

Of the twelve signs of the zodiac, three are fire signs (Aries, Leo, and Sagittarius), three water signs (Cancer, Scorpio, and Pisces), three air signs (Libra, Aquarius, and Gemini), and three earth signs (Capricorn, Taurus, and Virgo).

There being nine small cards in each suit, the first three cards in the series (the 2s, 3s, and 4s) are assigned to the *cardinal signs* of the zodiac, the second three cards in the series (the 5s, 6s, and 7s) are assigned to the *fixed signs*, and the final three cards in the series (the 8s, 9s, and 10s) are assigned to the *mutable signs*.

Here's how that works:

- The 2s, 3s, and 4s of each suit represent the *cardinal signs* of the zodiac, thus:
  - 2-3-4 of *Wands* = the 1st, 2nd, and 3rd decans of **Aries** *(cardinal fire)*

- 2-3-4 of *Cups* = the 1ˢᵗ, 2ⁿᵈ, and 3ʳᵈ decans of **Cancer** *(cardinal water)*
- 2-3-4 of *Swords* = the 1ˢᵗ, 2ⁿᵈ, and 3ʳᵈ decans of **Libra** *(cardinal air)*
- 2-3-4 of *Disks* = the 1ˢᵗ, 2ⁿᵈ, and 3ʳᵈ decans of **Capricorn** *(cardinal earth)*

- The 5s, 6s, and 7s of each suit represent the *fixed signs* of the zodiac, thus:
  - 5-6-7 of *Wands* = the 1ˢᵗ, 2ⁿᵈ, and 3ʳᵈ decans of **Leo** *(fixed fire)*
  - 5-6-7 of *Cups* = the 1ˢᵗ, 2ⁿᵈ, and 3ʳᵈ decans of **Scorpio** *(fixed water)*
  - 5-6-7 of *Swords* = the 1ˢᵗ, 2ⁿᵈ, and 3ʳᵈ decans of **Aquarius** *(fixed air)*
  - 5-6-7 of *Disks* = the 1ˢᵗ, 2ⁿᵈ, and 3ʳᵈ decans of **Taurus** *(fixed earth)*

- The 8s, 9s, and 10s of each suit represent the *mutable signs* of the zodiac, thus:
  - 8-9-10 of *Wands* = the 1ˢᵗ, 2ⁿᵈ, and 3ʳᵈ decans of **Sagittarius** *(mutable fire)*
  - 8-9-10 of *Cups* = the 1ˢᵗ, 2ⁿᵈ, and 3ʳᵈ decans of **Pisces** *(mutable water)*
  - 8-9-10 of *Swords* = the 1ˢᵗ, 2ⁿᵈ, and 3ʳᵈ decans of **Gemini** *(mutable air)*
  - 8-9-10 of *Disks* = the 1ˢᵗ, 2ⁿᵈ, and 3ʳᵈ decans of **Virgo** *(mutable earth)*

So, to create a complete, beautiful, and most proper homemade magick circle, simply clear a space on the floor and surround yourself with the thirty-six small cards of the Tarot laid out like this:

Starting in the east, lay the cards around you in a *counterclockwise* direction, just like the wheel of the zodiac:

Aries: 2 Wands, 3 Wands, 4 Wands

Taurus: 5 Disks, 6 Disks, 7 Disks

Gemini: 8 Swords, 9 Swords, 10 Swords

Cancer: 2 Cups, 3 Cups, 4 Cups

Leo: 5 Wands, 6 Wands, 7 Wands

Virgo: 8 Disks, 9 Disks, 10 Disks

Libra: 2 Swords, 3 Swords, 4 Swords

Scorpio: 5 Cups, 6 Cups, 7 Cups

Sagittarius: 8 Wands, 9 Wands, 10 Wands

Capricorn: 2 Disks, 3 Disks, 4 Disks

Aquarius: 5 Swords, 6 Swords, 7 Swords

Pisces: 8 Cups, 9 Cups, 10 Cups

Voila! An elegant, accurate, and functional magick circle.

When you think about it, the simple act of taking a well-shuffled deck of Tarot cards and reordering and reassembling them in neat and precise astrological order is, in and of itself, a magical exercise of the highest order. After all, how many opportunities do you get every day to take your "shuffled deck" (your screwed-up and unorganized life and universe) and put it in perfect order?

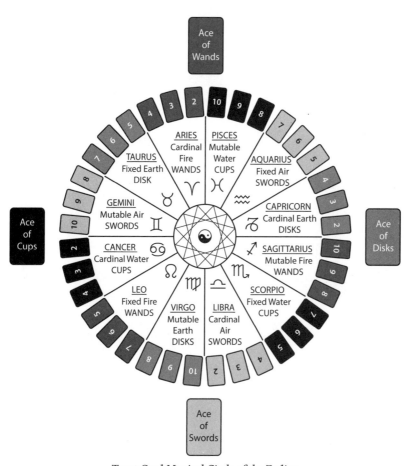

Tarot Card Magical Circle of the Zodiac

FOURTEEN

Challenges and Rewards of Being Married to Another Magician

A MARRIAGE SECRET

When two strong souls,
And two strong wills,
And two strong minds unite,
There will come rounds
When standing your grounds
Will turn in to a fight.

So here and now,
Before reciting your vows,
And while you're high as a kite,
Agree that one of you will know everything,
And the other will always be right.

This compromise
Is very wise,
You'll use it day and night.
It's an understanding
That's not demanding,
It's unbreakable, try as you might.

So leave behind
The undefined.
Step boldly into the light
Of a world where one of you knows everything,
And the other is always right.[47]

I don't know if the above sentiments are really the ultimate secret of marriage, but they certainly ring true in the DuQuette household. Constance and I discovered in the early days of our marriage that when we discuss (argue about) important matters, each of us contributes a unique and ultimately accurate assessment of the issue. I am usually armed with an arsenal of facts and objective observations, but I am quick to jump to conclusions and am inclined to pragmatically (or emotionally) surrender my ideals under the inescapable weight of objective reality. Constance, on the other hand, possesses the absolutely annoying ability to immediately grasp the deeper spiritual dimensions of any manifested issue or question. Furthermore, to make matters doubly infuriating, she has the guileless audacity to give perfect voice to the moral, spiritual, and philosophical truth underlying the entire situation. In other words, I may know everything, but she is *always right!*

A relationship such as ours could hardly be called serene, but when all is said and done, it has produced a life of profound serenity. I won't try to kid you. We argue. We argue a lot! Familiarity really *does* breed contempt, and so far we've enjoyed forty-seven years of familiarity. We argue because occasionally she actually needs to hear the cold hard facts

---

47. Lon Milo DuQuette, *Ask Baba Lon: Answers to Questions of Life and Magick* (Las Vegas, NV: New Falcon Publications, 2011), pp. 80–82.

and the perspective of a flawed and perpetually adolescent mortal, and I ultimately always need to hear the voice of God and understand what those cold hard facts actually mean to my soul.

Together, since 1978, Constance and I have directed the activities of a lodge of the O.T.O. We've organized, set up, performed, torn down, and cleaned up after hundreds of degree initiation ceremonies, Gnostic Masses, public rites, plays, and celebrations and literally thousands of classes and workshops. All of these events have taken place in classrooms, temples, and theaters created from the space and the furnishings of our home—from our living room, from our garage, from our backyard. End tables become altars and fonts, plant pedestals become ritual columns, and curtains become veils.

Getting ready for homemade magick can be exhausting. I have to confess that Constance does 99 percent of the hard work of setting up for our public events and lodge rituals. I caught her resting a moment on a shady coffin prior to a backyard Rite of Eleusis.

Constance as Scorpio-Apophis dances to Albinoni's *Adagio in D minor* and mourns the death and entombment of the sun god (played this year by our son, Jean-Paul) in this scene from a backyard performance of the Rite of Sol (from the Rites of Eleusis). The columns in the background are our living-room plant stands. The veil (barely visible) is strung between two backyard trees. The coffin was built by a lodge brother. On other occasions it has served as the tomb in the Gnostic Mass.

It's hard work, and because of her need for neatness and perfection (and because of my inherent laziness and sloppiness), Constance always ends up doing 99 percent of the physical labor involved. Each event is preceded by prolonged and spirited "discussions" (in which I know everything about one thing or another and she is always right). But from out of all the tension and conflict is born something very magical—a world rare and wonderful; a safe and relatively stable environment to raise our son; a cultural (or sub-cultural) atmosphere filled with stimulating conversation, art, music, and literature; a universe peopled with some of the most interesting, talented, brilliant, and colorful individuals in the world. Together our craziness has enriched and transformed our lives, and allowed two magicians with extremely different styles and temperaments the freedom to do our individual Great Work while sharing our lives and our love with the world.

Perhaps our most important collaboration has been the creation and presentation of "The Miracle of the Mass," our all-day public seminar on the O.T.O.'s Mass of the Gnostic Catholic Church (more commonly referred to simply as the Gnostic Mass). In the last twenty years, we have presented this seminar from Tokyo to Oslo and throughout the United States. It has recently been recorded and serialized on the Internet.

The Gnostic Mass is a ceremonial *tour de force* of sexual alchemy, and in many ways is one of the most beautiful and important contributions from Aleister Crowley to Western esotericism. It is quite frankly the essence of the mysteries of the Holy Grail. Our love for (and appreciation of) this ritual made our collaboration uncharacteristically civil, and our usual volatile chemistry transmuted to create a serious and authoritative commentary on the ceremony (in particular) and sex magick (in general).

Constance and I have yet to collaborate on a full book or musical project (which is perhaps a good thing). But in the early 1990s, we began collaboration on an art project that is likely to last long after we have both moved on to our next incarnational adventures. I'm talking about the Tarot of Ceremonial Magick, our deck of Tarot cards. I believe there is perhaps no more perfect example of the challenges, tribulations, and rewards of a homemade magick operation than the story of the creation and eventual publication of this deck of cards.

FIFTEEN

Homemade Tarot Cards

One could say that the Tarot is the DNA of the Qabalah. Properly
decoded it reveals not only the secrets of the Qabalah but also the mys-
teries of all other Qabalah-based systems ... By learning Tarot properly
you simultaneously master the fundamentals of Qabalah, Astrology and
Ceremonial Magick.

CONSTANCE AND LON DUQUETTE,
IN THE BOOKLET TO THE TAROT OF CEREMONIAL MAGICK

In chapter 13, I discussed how, whenever I'm away from home, I can construct a homemade magick temple and circle using Tarot cards. The cards
that I carry with me (indeed, the cards that I use exclusively for personal
and professional readings) are my own homemade ones from the Tarot
of Ceremonial Magick. I designed and penned the line drawings for each
of the seventy-eight cards, and Constance painted them in watercolor. Together we wrote the little booklet that accompanies the deck. It was quite
literally a family project.

First of all, I did not set out to create a Tarot deck. I simply wanted
to make a handmade set of flashcards for Monday Night Magick Class.

I accidentally found myself a job as office manager for a stockbroker in San Juan Capistrano. (How I secured that position is a story in itself.) My boss was a wonderful and brilliant and successful man whose clients were wealthy Orange County physicians. He was usually out of the office, and most days I only saw him in the morning and late afternoon. I had plenty of typing, filing, and marketing duties to complete, but I also had quite a lot of time each day to study, write, or get ready for class.

At the time, we were studying the magical tables of correspondences in Crowley's *Liber 777,*[48] and I was preparing to discuss the particular sets of tables that demonstrate how certain traditional qabalistic angels and demons are assigned to the thirty-six decans of the zodiac in the same way that the thirty-six small cards of the Tarot are assigned to those same decans. I thought it would be nice if each member could have thirty-six blank notecards so that we, as a class, could transfer the information from the tables to the cards.

We started by labeling the thirty-six cards by degrees (decans) of the zodiac: (0°–10° Aries), (10°–20° Aries), (20°–30° Aries), (0°–10° Taurus), (10°–20° Taurus), (20°–30° Taurus), etc.

We then added the approximate ten days of the year that those decans represent. We used red ink for the cards of the fire signs of the zodiac, blue for the water signs, yellow for the air signs, and green for the earth signs.

After the first class, each member had a nice neat stack of cards representing the entire astrological year. The following week we added more information from the tables of correspondences, specifically the qabalistic angels of the Shemhamphoras and the Goetic demons assigned to the decans of the zodiac. We carefully placed the names of these angels and the names and seals of the demons on the appropriate cards.

The next week we added the planetary assignments to each of our thirty-six decan cards, plus their Tarot card suit and number. Beginning at 0 degrees Leo and working our way around the Wheel of the Year, we assigned planets to the decans in a repeating order of Saturn, Jupiter, Mars, Sun, Venus, Mercury, and Moon. (Mars was repeated at the last wintertime decan of Pisces and the first springtime decan of Aries.)

---

48. Aleister Crowley, *777 and Other Qabalistic Writings* (York Beach, ME: Weiser Books, 1986).

The notecard project provided our class members with a wonderful introduction to the fundamentals of astrology, but we needed to move on to other subjects. I, however, was hooked. I knew that if I proceeded, I would have the makings of a unique and magical Tarot deck. I bought a case of 4 x 6-inch unruled white index cards and used my spare time at work experimenting with formatting images for the cards. This was in the late 1980s, before the availability of more advanced computer imaging, so I had to do everything with plastic transparencies, a copy machine, and a word processor. I eventually included appropriate images and information from Enochian magick and the I Ching, where those systems correspond to the Tarot.

The preliminary work took two years to complete. The original art consisted of my seventy-eight uncolored line drawings printed one at a time with a standard office copy machine on ordinary white index cards.

In order to be *qabalistically correct*, each trump and the cards of each suit had to conform to a strict color scale. Each zodiac sign, each planet, each elemental suit, and each *number* of each suit vibrates at a specific frequency on the color spectrum, and all these factors needed to be considered when selecting and blending the colors of any given card. I was, frankly, burned out on the project and did not feel up to the task.

Constance, on the other hand, is a fantastic artist. Throughout our years of marriage, she has amused us all with her ink drawings, pencil sketches, and crayon and watercolor paintings. Her eye for color is precise and tasteful. She did not, however, jump up to volunteer to help with this project.

Then I got an early-evening call from my dear friend and former boss, Rick Potter. He was planning to drive to Miami to attend the American Booksellers Association trade show (now called BookExpo America) and asked if I'd like to go along for the ride. He was leaving in ten days. It would be the perfect opportunity for me to pitch my Tarot deck, but an uncolored Tarot deck would not be very impressive, no matter how "correct" it was.

Later that night, the after-dinner conversation went something like this:

"Oh, by the way, Rick called today and said he's driving his new Mercedes to Miami to attend the booksellers convention. He wants to know if I'd like to ride along, maybe spend a couple days in New Orleans on the way. He says we would only be gone twenty days or so. My publishers would really like it if I could spend a little time at their booths."

Constance, while not overly enthusiastic about such an adventure, was nonetheless generally supportive of the whole idea.

I added, "You know, while I'm there, I could pitch my Tarot cards to U.S. Games Systems and maybe get Weiser to publish my new book on the cards."

She looked at me funny. "What book?"

"The one I'll write if they publish the cards."

"But you haven't colored the cards yet."

The next part took real magical finesse.

"I thought I'd give you a couple of color scale charts and let you take a crack at coloring in the cards. Should be a piece of cake for you."

"All seventy-eight cards?"

"That's right."

"How long do I have?"

"Ten days … well … nine."

"That'd be about nine cards a day."

"Yeah. If you did a couple tonight, it would be more like eight a day."

The clocks stopped ticking, the crickets stopped chirping, the dog stopped panting, and I stopped breathing.

"Okay. Show me those charts."

Bless her heart, she did it, too. Right on time. Rick and I drove from Newport Beach, California, to Miami, and I successfully pitched and inked the card deal with U.S. Games Systems and the book deal with Weiser.

The moment I arrived back home, Constance and I set to work on writing the little book that accompanies the cards, including her wise (and patently un-Lon-like) insights on the divinatory meanings of each card of our homemade Tarot deck.

Our Tarot cards are much like our marriage: beautiful in some areas and not so beautiful in others, homemade, and magically correct.

Color Scales for the Aces and Small Cards of the Tarot

Key Scale	Card Number	Sephirah	King Scale WANDS	Queen Scale CUPS	Prince Scale SWORDS	Princess Scale DISKS
1	Ace	Kether	Brilliance	White brilliance	White brilliance	White flecked gold
2	Two	Chokmah	Pure soft blue	Gray	Blue pearl gray, like mother-of-pearl	White flecked red, blue, and yellow
3	Three	Binah	Crimson	Black	Dark brown	Gray flecked pink
4	Four	Chesed	Deep violet	Blue	Deep purple	Deep azure flecked yellow
5	Five	Geburah	Orange	Scarlet red	Bright scarlet	Red flecked black
6	Six	Tiphareth	Clear pink rose	Yellow (gold)	Rich salmon	Gold amber
7	Seven	Netzach	Amber	Emerald	Bright yellow green	Olive flecked gold
8	Eight	Hod	Violet	Orange	Red-russet	Yellowish-brown flecked white
9	Nine	Yesod	Indigo	Violet	Very dark purple	Citrine flecked azure
10	Ten	Malkuth	Yellow	Citrine (N), olive (E), russet (W), and black (S)—saltire (forming an X)*	As Queen Scale but gold flecked black	Black rayed yellow

*Citrine combines blue, red, and yellow, with a predominance of yellow: olive, with a predominance of blue; and russet, with a predominance of red; and these represent, respectively, the airy, watery, and fiery sub-elements. Black is the earthy part of earth.

Color Scales for the Trumps of the Tarot

Key Scale	Trump Number	Trump Title and Attribute	King Scale	Queen Scale	Prince Scale	Princess Scale
11	0	The Fool (Air)	Bright pale yellow	Sky blue	Blue emerald green	Emerald flecked gold
12	1	The Magus (Mercury)	Yellow	Purple	Gray	Indigo rayed violet
13	2	The High Priestess (Moon)	Blue	Silver	Cold pale blue	Silver rayed sky blue
14	3	The Empress (Venus)	Emerald green	Sky blue	Early spring green	Rose or cerise rayed pale green
28	4	The Emperor (Aries)	Scarlet	Red	Brilliant flame	Glowing red
16	5	The Hierophant (Taurus)	Red orange	Deep indigo	Deep warm olive	Rich brown
17	6	The Lovers (Gemini)	Orange	Pale mauve	New yellow leather	Reddish gray inclined to mauve
18	7	The Chariot (Cancer)	Amber	Maroon	Rich bright russet	Dark greenish brown
22	8	Adjustment (Libra)	Emerald green	Blue	Deep blue-green	Pale green
20	9	The Hermit (Virgo)	Green (yellowish)	Slate gray	Green gray	Plum
21	10	Wheel of Fortune (Jupiter)	Violet	Blue	Rich purple	Bright blue rayed yellow
19	11	Lust (Leo)	Yellow (greenish)	Deep purple	Gray	Reddish amber

Color Scales for the Trumps of the Tarot (cont.)

Key Scale	Trump Number	Trump Title and Attribute	King Scale	Queen Scale	Prince Scale	Princess Scale
23	12	The Hanged Man (Water)	Deep blue	Sea-green	Deep olive green	White flecked purple
24	13	Death (Scorpio)	Green blue	Dull brown	Very dark brown	Vivid indigo brown
25	14	Art (Sagittarius)	Blue	Yellow	Green	Dark vivid blue
26	15	The Devil (Capricorn)	Indigo	Black	Blue-black	Cold, dark gray nearing black
27	16	The Tower (Mars)	Scarlet	Red	Venetian red	Bright red rayed azure or emerald
15	17	The Star (Aquarius)	Violet	Sky blue	Bluish mauve	White tinged purple
29	18	The Moon (Pisces)	Crimson (ultra-violet)	Buff flecked silver white	Light translucent pinkish Brown	Stone
30	19	The Sun (Sun)	Orange	Gold yellow	Rich amber	Amber rayed red
31	20	The Aeon (Fire)	Glowing orange scarlet	Vermilion	Scarlet flecked gold	Vermilion flecked crimson and emerald
32	21	The Universe (Saturn)	Indigo	Black	Blue-black	Black rayed blue
32	21	The Universe (Earth)	Citrine, olive, russet, and black	Amber	Dark brown	Black flecked yellow
31	20	The Aeon (Spirit)	White merging into gray	Deep purple nearly black	7 prismatic colors (violet outside)	White, red, yellow, blue, black (this on outside)

SIXTEEN

Do I Have
to Get a Job?

The first task of the magician is to master his or her immediate envi-
ronment ... On the mundane plane this means the ability to provide
materially for yourself and your family (if that is your situation) in
such a manner as to allow you to also pursue your spiritual disciplines.
This is no mean task, and I doff my magical cap to anyone who can
achieve such a lifestyle.[49]

In 1993 I was sitting in my underwear at my computer typing away at a
new book when Jean-Paul noticed how fast I was typing and suggested
that could I apply at a local employment agency and easily get a few temporary office jobs. I told him that such agencies didn't want fat, middle-
aged men, but that I'd think about it.

---

49. Lon Milo DuQuette, *The Magick of Aleister Crowley* (York Beach, ME: Weiser
Books, 2003), p. 52.

Properly shamed into action by my own son (and to prove my inherent incapacity to secure honest work), I decided I would at least give it a try. I put on a suit and tie and hopped on my little motor scooter and headed off to the nearest agency. To my surprise, they were absolutely thrilled at my typing speed and downright giddy over my mastery of the English alphabet and the fact that I could speak in complete sentences. They immediately signed me up and sent me off to a job in a posh office building in Newport Beach.

The company was a small, five-person branch office of a commercial real-estate firm that negotiated on behalf of tenants in the process of securing new facilities. I didn't understand a thing about the business, but I soon discovered I could type everyone's letters, organize their files, and generally manage the office while half-asleep and still have about five hours a day left over to quietly sit in my cubicle and secretly work on my next book. Everyone was happy with my work, so after a month or so they "bought" me from the temporary agency and made me part of the family.

I couldn't believe my good fortune. I was actually being paid each day to write my own books. The company was doing well also—so good, in fact, that we were soon acquired by a much larger and more celebrated commercial real-estate company. I feared I wouldn't be able to keep up the charade for long under the scrutiny of new management, but before I could be found out, the new company was acquired by an even larger and more celebrated global real-estate institution. I and my five old "bosses" moved to a gleaming new building overlooking the Newport Beach Back Bay.

As luck would have it, the new organization was so big that nobody knew exactly who I was or what exactly I did there. I still typed up a few letters and did some filing for my pals from the old company, but for the most part I became quite invisible. I had no supervisor and no *supervision*.

Every day for the next nine years, I arrived to work, dressed smartly in the obligatory white shirt and tie. Every day for the next nine years, I expected to be unmasked as an impostor and fired. I wrote six books[50] in those nine years—at work.

Eventually, because of my exemplary work habits (always busy—arriving early and staying late) but mostly because of my silver hair (which made me look incredibly distinguished and competent), I was asked by the director of the accounting department (who regularly had me read her Tarot cards) if I could make time in my busy day to help handle the firm's checks and bank wire transfers, along with the necessary documentation.

This was finally starting to look like a real job, and indeed, my last couple of years with the firm actually gave me the opportunity to do some honest work and assuaged a bit of my guilt. I confess, however, that I was somewhat relieved when the company ultimately merged with the largest firm of its kind in the world and I saw my opportunity to take, as it were, "early retirement." In 2003 I put on my modest "parachute," stepped out of the corporate airplane, and plunged into the next phase of my life as a *full-time Lon.*

Since 2003 I have been home all day long—and as much as we love each other, Constance and I have discovered that we can occasionally get on each other's nerves. One morning she woke me up and said, "Let's play monastery!" and I said, "Yes! Let's do!"

---

50. *Magick of Thelema, Tarot of Ceremonial Magick, My Life with the Spirits, Angels Demons and Gods of the New Millennium, Accidental Christ,* and *Understanding Aleister Crowley's Thoth Tarot.*

SEVENTEEN

Homemade Monastery

My imagination is a monastery and I am its monk.
JOHN KEATS

Let me begin this chapter by telling you that throughout our forty-seven-year (so far) marriage, Constance and I have both routinely performed yogic and magical exercises and meditations. In our hippie days in Southern Oregon, we observed regular days of fasting and silence. We each have our own household altars and meditation areas. We each have our own personal mantras, prayers, and rituals that we use before meals, at bedtime, and upon arising.

Daily spiritual practices and disciplines are nothing new to us, so when Constance suggested we play monastery, I enthusiastically agreed to do it. We kept up the program for nearly three years.

Did it help our magick or our marriage? We can't say for certain. But we are still magicians ... and we are still married.

The homemade altar of Saint Constance. We have a tiny loft in our home that serves as our library and guest bedroom. It is also where Constance meditates each morning after doing tai chi in the garden. The altar honors a broad assortment of our household gods, patron saints, and sacred objects.

———

RULE OF THE MONASTERY OF SAINT CONSTANCE

Sunrise Resh

We adore the sun at dawn by standing together, facing east, and reciting the morning section of *Liber Resh,*[51] a solar adoration recommended for daily use by Thelemic magicians.

> *Hail unto Thee who art Ra in Thy rising, even unto Thee who art Ra in Thy strength, who travellest over the Heavens in Thy bark at the Uprising of the Sun. Tahuti standeth in His splendour at the prow, and Ra-Hoor abideth at the helm. Hail unto Thee from the Abodes of Night!*

---

51. *Liber Resh vel Helios sub Figura CC* is also found in its entirety in Aleister Crowley's *The Equinox*, vol. 1, no. 6 (Reprint, York Beach, ME: Samuel Weiser, 1990).

Morning Bell

Constance rings the bell. (Our bell is a small brass bell we've used in personal rituals since we were first married. We're very sentimental about these things.)

Morning Period of Silence

The ringing of the bell signals a period of complete silence. Any communication between us is strictly nonverbal. The silent period usually lasts from two to three hours until breakfast is prepared and we are ready to eat. Until then, we proceed with our morning devotions in strict silence. (If you've never tried this, it is not only relaxing but oddly liberating. If nothing else, it quickly proves just how much of our daily chatter is completely useless, unproductive, and hurtful.)

Morning Devotions

After taking turns in the bathroom, we begin our morning devotions. Constance begins by lighting a stick of incense and, moving through the entire house in a clockwise direction, censing and blessing each room. The censing is accompanied by a profoundly simple ceremony— a breathing technique she developed whereby she *projects* her love with each exhalation of her breath, and *accepts* the love of the universe with each inhalation.

The house duly blessed (and smelling great), she then retires upstairs to the loft (which also serves as my library), where she has a small floor altar set up. There she lights a candle and sits down to perform pranayama.[52] She ends her devotional period each morning by reading from what she calls her "desert island" books.[53]

Constance then stands up and opens the loft window and blesses the entire neighborhood and the world. Then she blows out the candle and

---

52. Breath-control exercises, followed by a period of meditation.

53. For most of our monastery years, these texts included *The Holy Books of Thelema* by Aleister Crowley, *The Treasure House of Images* by J. F. C. Fuller, *Metaphysical Meditations* by Paramahansa Yogananda, and *The Art of Peace* by Morihei Ueshiba.

goes downstairs to do laundry, feed the cat, and make our breakfast. I told you she was a saint.

While Constance does her thing in the house, I take my morning devotionals to the backyard patio. There I perform (for all the neighbors to witness) a not-so-quiet banishing pentagram ritual. I then do a few stretches and sit down for a period of pranayama, followed by mentally chanting a mantra that I have adopted. (During the three years we played monastery, my daily routine expanded and evolved considerably. My banishing developed into a combined ceremony of invocation and banishing that I use to this day.)

My meditations continue until I hear the bell ring, which signals the end of the period of silence and breakfast.

Breakfast

Constance insists (and who am I to argue with Saint Constance?) that we eat breakfast outside in the patio area of our backyard. (We do this every day. The only exception to this is when it is raining *hard*. If it is just very cold or just sprinkling, we eat outside.)

Will

Before eating, we break our period of silence by saying "Will"[54] over our food.

One of us knocks 11 times (3-5-3) with our knife (or spoon or chop stick) and says, *Do what thou wilt shall be the whole of the Law.*

The other asks, *What is thy will?*

The first replies, *It is my will to eat and drink.*

The other asks, *To what end?*

The first replies, *That my body may be fortified thereby.*

The other asks, *To what end?*

The first replies, *That I may accomplish the Great Work.*

Then both say together, *Love is the law, love under will.*

The first ends by saying, *Fall to!* and knocks once to end the ritual.

---

54. Will is the classic Thelemic meal-blessing ceremony.

After breakfast we go about our day as we normally would if we were not playing monastery, pausing only to say *Resh* at noon, sunset, and midnight, and saying "Will" before our meals.

Noon Resh

At noon or as close as possible, we stand together, facing south, and say:

Hail unto Thee who art Ahathoor in Thy triumphing, even unto Thee who art Ahathoor in Thy beauty, who travellest over the heavens in thy bark at the Mid-course of the Sun. Tahuti standeth in His splendour at the prow, and Ra-Hoor abideth at the helm. Hail unto Thee from the Abodes of Morning!

Sunset Resh

At sunset or as close as possible we stand together, facing west, and say:

Hail unto Thee who art Tum in Thy setting, even unto Thee who art Tum in Thy joy, who travellest over the Heavens in Thy bark at the Down-going of the Sun. Tahuti standeth in His splendour at the prow, and Ra-Hoor abideth at the helm. Hail unto Thee from the Abodes of Day!

Midnight Resh

At midnight or as close as possible, we stand together, facing north, and say:

Hail unto thee who art Khephra in Thy hiding, even unto Thee who art Khephra in Thy silence, who travellest over the heavens in Thy bark at the Midnight Hour of the Sun. Tahuti standeth in His splendour at the prow, and Ra-Hoor abideth at the helm. Hail unto Thee from the Abodes of Evening.

We played monastery like this for nearly three years, during which time our individual disciplines and devotional practices evolved considerably. Most dramatically, Constance incorporated tai chi chih to her morning practices and I began walking—seriously walking. In doing so, I lost 150 pounds and most likely extended my life.

EIGHTEEN

The Demon
Who Saved My Life

> *Their faces and their shapes are terrible and strange.*
> *These devils by my might to angels I will change.*
> *These nameless horrors I address without affright:*
> *On them will I impose my will, the law of light.*
> ELIPHAS LEVI[55]

In the 1940s and 1950s, the demon polio was sweeping over the planet, killing and paralyzing over a half million people each year in a nightmarish epidemic that threatened to dwarf the horrors of any world war. Many of its victims were children, and by 1951, when I was three years old, the disease had already claimed the lives of neighborhood boys and girls on all sides of our modest home in Lakewood, California. I can only imagine

---

55. "The Magician," translated from Eliphas Levi's version of the famous hymn. Published in *The Equinox,* vol. 1, no. 1 (1909, Reprint: York Beach, ME: Samuel Weiser, 1992), p. 109.

the terror that seized my parents' hearts when, only a few months after I took my first steps, I complained of pain in my legs and found it difficult to walk.

To everyone's relief, I didn't have polio. But I was diagnosed with a serious bone disease called Perthes hip[56] and was immediately immobilized and forbidden to walk or exercise below the waist. In an attempt to chemically mellow me out while lying on my back for the next few years, I was prescribed what were generically called "thyroid pills." The pills must have worked, because I learned to absolutely wallow in the delights of quiet contemplation and physical inactivity. Unfortunately, the medication did nothing to curb my appetite (or the insecurities of youth) and I quickly fell into what would become a lifelong struggle with my weight.

By the time I was five, I was walking with crutches, and a year or so after that, I was allowed to walk on my own, but no running or jumping was allowed. At the age of fourteen, and after countless x-rays (that are probably responsible for the growth of my superfluous third nipple and the seventh toe on my left foot[57]), I was pronounced "cured" of Perthes disease, but with an ominous caveat from my doctor, who wrinkled his brow and told my mother I'd better secure a sedentary desk job by the time I was thirty or I'd be crippled for the rest of my life.

A "sedentary" lifestyle sounded great to me. I loved not moving around, and by my late teens, my body's metabolism was happy just to kick back, relax, and convert my food's energy almost directly into fat. Things didn't get really bad, however, until the mid-1980s, when a painful and permanent back injury, a string of comfy desk jobs, my new writing

---

56. The American Academy of Orthopedic Surgeons describes Perthes as "a condition in children characterized by a temporary loss of blood supply to the hip. Without an adequate blood supply, the rounded head of the femur (the 'ball' of the 'ball and socket' joint of the hip) dies. The area becomes intensely inflamed and irritated. Treatment of Perthes may require periods of immobilization or limitations on usual activities. The long-term prognosis is good in most cases. After 18 months to 2 years of treatment, most children return to normal activities without major limitations."

57. Just kidding.

career, and a crippling injury that severed my Achilles tendon encouraged me to surrender completely to the great-tasting demon *obesity*.

I invoked this gargantuan demon with the following ritual. Each weekday I got up at 3:00 am and wrote until I left for work at 7:30 am. I drank way too much coffee at work. Then I ate too much lunch to ease the coffee jitters. After work I religiously stopped at my neighborhood liquor store and bought two canned martinis, which I knocked back as I drove blissfully around the beautiful Newport Back Bay. Then, after watching a breathtaking sunset over Catalina Island, I arrived home for a great dinner (of which I ate far too much), then fell blissfully asleep on a full stomach.

I knew this cycle of behavior was killing me, but it was the structured rhythm that drove one of the most remarkably productive and creative periods of my entire life. While it lasted, it was damn near heaven. Heaven, however, came at a *heavy* price. I blew up to 310 pounds and the *elephant in the room* that nobody was talking about … *was me.*

That's not quite true. I would discover that there *was* someone talking about the elephant in the room—a *demon*. Actually, the demon was (is) a real person, a mean-spirited and well-read magical blogger who actually had the brash *audacity* to publish his[58] openly hostile opinions about Lon Milo DuQuette.

Naturally, I would like everybody in the world to love me, but I know that's not going to happen. People who are passionate about magick have very strong opinions about what it all means. Magick is an art, and artists are often odd, eccentric, and antisocial people. I'm used to fielding questions, suggestions, and criticisms from some pretty odd individuals, some of whom have been living far too long in their mother's basement. However, most people who feel impelled to bring my name into the discussion, even when they disagree with me, are generally gracious and polite.

This guy was a real jerk!

What really hurt, though, was that every hurtful word he wrote about me in his hateful blogs had some measure of truth in it. He was actually

---

58. I have assumed this person was/is a man. At least the various pseudonyms under which this person posts on the Internet suggest it is a man.

seeing me as accurately as he could from where he was standing. Irritating as he was, I developed a perverse liking and respect for the guy.

Somehow he got my private e-mail address and wrote to me directly. It was obvious he wanted to pick a magical fight that he could later blog about. The letter was a thinly disguised probe for a quote—asking me one of those impossible-to-answer *pharisee-esque* trick questions of philosophy. Not wishing to take the bait and enmesh myself in some emotionally charged argument over the finer points of Qabalah or the objective reality of Satan, I replied as politely and truthfully as I could. I'm sure my response frustrated him to no end, for it gave him no opening to continue an argument.

Then, after a few months of no communication, he dropped all pretense of civility and wrote me a very rude and insulting message. Like a schoolyard bully who has run out of witty excuses to pick a fight with the class nerd, he resorted simply to ridiculing my physical appearance.

He quoted my own words, *The only thing I can change with magick is myself,* and suggested that if I really believed that, why didn't I use my magick to evoke the spirits of *diet* and *exercise* to change myself from the grotesque, fat, and bloated monster I had allowed myself to grow into?

Now, I'm a pretty thick-skinned guy, but you can probably imagine how much those words hurt and upset me. I found myself hating this fellow with a passion that I'm sure eclipsed his hatred for me a thousand-fold. But then something very odd happened that immediately caused me to stop hating him. I even stopped being mad and irritated by him. I realized that despite the fact that this individual was a pathetic and hate-poisoned bully, he was absolutely right! He wasn't a lying spirit. He was the angel of truth—the omniscient voice of God.

Constance had for years urged me to heed her informed advice concerning diet and exercise, but did I listen to my angel? No! It took the hateful and unkind words of this *asshole*—this demon—to finally get the message through this thick skull of mine and snap me out of my suicidal nightmare. I finally admitted to myself that if my sedentary lifestyle and poor eating habits continued, I would soon face the deadly consequences of diabetes, heart disease, and death. The demon blogger opened my eyes to the truth that I could change it all with one profoundly simple magical act.

I only needed do one thing: obey Constance!

She immediately put me on a nutritional supplement program and removed from my diet alcohol, sugar (and things that turn to sugar in the body), most breads, and dairy products. I replaced fried foods and junk with whole grains and ten to twelve servings of fruits and vegetables a day. Almost immediately I started feeling better, sleeping better, and thinking better.

Then I started to walk. At first I could walk only a few yards down the street before the crippling pain in my back sent me howling back into the house. Each day I walked a few steps farther down the street. Then I walked twice a day, each time a little farther. The first day I walked completely around the block, I celebrated with a big glass of Green Magma.

Day after day I walked farther away from home and the pain in my back became more tolerable. Each day I watched my shadow on the sidewalk grow thinner and thinner. After six months on the Saint Constance Health and Beauty Program, I went to the doctor for a long overdue examination and blood work. All my numbers were better than normal—blood pressure, glucose, cholesterol, everything.

My daily routine now includes walking five miles a day (half in the morning, half in the afternoon or evening), a heroic vitamin and nutritional supplement program (which includes mushroom supplements that have corrected my metabolism), and eating whatever Saint Constance prepares for me. I lost 150 pounds and have maintained my weight at 160 pounds for the last three years.

Did I lose 150 pounds with magick?

You're damn right I did it with magick! And I did it with the divine assistance of an angel who loves me and a perfectly unpleasant demon who hates my guts (only now, it seems he has less to hate). I honor them both and thank them from the bottom of my heart.

NINETEEN

Backyard Mystery School

*In the Jewish, Christian, and Islamic religions we think of God not only
as a monarch but as the maker of the world, and, as a result of that,
we look upon the world as an artifact, a sort of machine, created by a
greet engineer. There's a different conception in India, where the world
is not seen as an artifact, but as a drama. And therefore God is not the
maker and architect of the universe but the actor of it, and is playing all
the parts at once, and this connects up with the idea of each one of us
as persons, because a person is a mask from the Latin persona, the mask
worn by the actors in Greco-Roman drama.*

ALAN WATTS[59]

Hippolyta: *This is the silliest stuff that ever I heard.*
Theseus: *The best in this kind are but shadows;
and the worst are no worse, if imagination amend them.*
WILLIAM SHAKESPEARE, *A MIDSUMMER NIGHT'S DREAM*, ACT 5, SCENE I

---

59. Alan Watts, *The Essential Alan Watts* (Berkeley, CA: Celestial Arts, 1977), p. 58.

There was a time when the term "home theater" meant the staging of an actual play in the parlor of one's own home. The vision harkens back to a quieter age before radio or television—to the genteel domesticity of Victorian *Little Women* in painted mustaches brandishing paper swords from atop a piano-bench pirate ship—a time when even grown-ups knew how to pretend and were not afraid to put on silly hats and be a king or a queen or a villain for an evening. Such magick penetrates deeper into our genetic history than the nineteenth century. All magick started as drama, and all drama started in the home.

Our homemade sun (son) god with (his mother) Scorpio-Apophis. Preparing for another backyard Rite of Sol, c. 1989. This was the second or third year Jean-Paul volunteered to play the part of the martyred sun god. It looks here like he's thinking of retiring the role.

———

Constance and I have been turning our home into a theater since 1978. The O.T.O. degree initiation ceremonies and Gnostic Masses are fully costumed and elaborate affairs, sometimes requiring several rooms furnished with heavy, custom-made pieces of equipment and paraphernalia. In 1982 we expanded our roles as magical impresarios and added the Rites of Eleusis to our playbill. Eventually we added to our repertoire the Rite of Earth, which forms the last section of this book.

But before we look at the rite itself, I'd like to offer some practical hints as to how almost anyone can mount a rather elaborate dramatic ritual presentation in their own home or apartment. It's a lot of work, but it's also a lot of fun, and it is (or can be) magick of the highest order.

Our magical rites didn't start out as magical rites at all. In fact, they started for us as an informal gathering of friends. One summer we simply invited a dozen or so friends over to celebrate the summer solstice with a potluck dinner party in our backyard. After everyone was sated and mellow, I gave each of our unsuspecting guests a script for Shakespeare's *A Midsummer Night's Dream*. (I made the booklets of this delightful comedy by copying them from my own old volume of Shakespeare, then printing and stapling them at work when no one was watching. I also carefully "highlighted" each script so it could be easily read by each individual character.)

We poured each "actor" another glass of wine and lit some torches and candles. Then I assigned[60] each confused partier a part and we were off! In short order, everyone was bitten by the thespian bug, and we discovered hidden talents in our friends that we never dreamed were there. The play was a roaring success! Everyone insisted we do it again the following year. After this informal read-through production, we knew we could do even more with our wonderful friends, and for the next twelve years or so, we did quite a bit more.

"Children, what is your will with me?" From the performance of a dining-room Rite of Saturn, c. 1985.

---

60. Somebody needs to be the director. In magick, it better be you.

Constance, as Mater Cœli (Mother of Heaven), has just been pulled through the veil of the Abyss by Brother Aquarius to aid in the invocation of the Master of the Temple (Saturn—me), who is still hidden behind the veil. Once I come out, I will recite the very scary Crowley poem "Dead Pharaoh's Eyes" while standing before the flaming bowl of alcohol. I love this stuff!

———

As Aries looks on, Soror Scorpio crowns Mars. Note the signs of Aries and Scorpio on the thrones on either side of Mars. For this performance, Mars is played by David P. Wilson (S. Jason Black). From the Rite of Mars, c. 1986.

———

OUTDOORS

Some dramatic rituals can be presented outside, and our backyards have been the scene of many. Naturally the weather needs to cooperate, but when it does, yard space is preferable to the cramped quarters of your living room or garage.

The stage can be anywhere you want it to be, preferably in a well-lit area of the yard and easily visible to a maximum number of people. If the ritual is done in the daylight hours, it is of course preferable that the audience sit in the shade. If there is no shaded area for them, set up temporary awnings or issue umbrellas.

If the ceremony requires veils (and many of them do), they can be strung on wires running between trees (and buildings) or between simply constructed poles. Perhaps the most simple and elegant way to "veil" a scene is by using two robed volunteers to hold up a length of colored fabric. These two volunteers also serve as the left and right columns of the proscenium arch of your stage.

Different locations and scenes can be represented by the placement of simple bits of "furniture." For outdoor ceremonies, a garden birdbath can be a river, an ocean, an oasis, or a garden, and a garden pedestal can be a temple or a castle. Potted plants and trees can be moved around to demarcate different scenes within the rite.

Finally, what about the neighbors?

You, of course, will want to be a good neighbor. If your neighbors can easily see and hear what's going on in your backyard, you will need to limit your events to those that are not secret, proprietary, or degree-sensitive to a particular society, order, or organization. Also, if you have little or no privacy from the neighbors, it is wise not to include elements of profanity, nudity, or overly loud music.

Like it or not, it is probably best to inform your neighbors in advance that you are having a gathering of friends and are going to be putting on a little homemade play. In fact, it is polite *and proper* that you actually invite them to the event. That can be a little scary, but chances are very slim that they will accept your invitation, and even if they do, the world will probably not end if they see a well-organized (if completely incomprehensible) play in the neighbor's backyard. Chances are they will just enjoy the beer.

Once we got serious about mounting homemade dramatic rituals, we turned to the Rites of Eleusis, which are a series of seven ritual dramas written by Aleister Crowley, each focusing on the character and mythology of one of the seven planetary gods of antiquity (Saturn, Jupiter,

Mars, Sol, Venus, Mercury, and Luna). In 1910 Crowley publicly presented the ceremonies for the first time at Caxton Hall in London, where they were generally well received. They did not spring Minerva-like and fully formed from Crowley's brain, however. They started quite demurely as an evening of homemade theater.

"In my heart is fidelity, fidelity, fidelity!" A square of red cloth thrown over a plain white robe makes a comfortable and passable toga. Add a broom-handle lance and voilà! Instant Brother Leo for a backyard Rite of Sol.

Crowley and his disciple Miss Leila Waddell (a professional violinist) had just enjoyed a quiet dinner at the home of a friend, and volunteered to entertain their host and the other guests with a little poetry and music. Over cognac and cigars, Crowley recited one of his poems, then Leila played her violin. Everyone seemed to enjoy the duel of verse and music, so they each did another round. Crowley observed a tangible change in consciousness in the mellow and sated audience that swung wildly depending on the energy and character of the particular poem or musical

piece. Before the evening was over, Crowley was convinced that he had
discovered the secret formula of the great mystery schools of antiquity—
that theater, music, poetry, and dance could be used to profoundly alter
and elevate human consciousness. He went home and immediately started to write the prototype ritual that would eventually become the Rites of
Eleusis.[61]

The Rites of Eleusis are not plays per se. The action is not driven by a
clearly recognizable plot. One immediately observes that the poetry, music, and dance numbers don't always have a direct connection to the mythological theme of the rite. The primary goal of the ceremony is instead
to create a specific kind of mood, reverie, or trance in the consciousness
of the individual members of the audience. If you feel melancholy and
depressed at the conclusion of the Rite of Saturn, good! If you are happy
and in a generous mood after the Rite of Jupiter, good! If you are in love
and a little horny after Venus, perfect!

Largely due to the efforts of newly organized O.T.O. bodies in California, the Rites of Eleusis were resurrected in the late 1970s, and our lodge
mounted the entire series every year throughout most of the 1980s. They
were very popular and gave us the opportunity to introduce magick (and
our lodge) to a larger community. Everyone involved found themselves
transformed in some way by the experience.

In 1985, while preparing for yet another season of the rites, someone suggested that it would be nice (and magically appropriate) if we
added at the conclusion of the series a *Rite of Earth*, to bring us all the
way down the Tree of Life to Malkuth—to ground us and properly seal
our efforts for the year. The myth of the earth goddess Demeter and her
daughter Persephone seemed like the ideal theme for such a ceremony;
after all, this was the central myth of the ancient Eleusinian mysteries.
So, completely ignoring my lack of talent for such things, I set to work
to assemble a homemade Rite of Earth.

I say "assemble" because I did not actually need to write very much
of the Rite of Earth. I simply started with the classic story, which I drew

61. Aleister Crowley, "The Rites of Eleusis," first published in *The Equinox*, vol. 1,
no. 6 (1911; Reprint, York Beach, ME: Weiser Books, 1992).

from an old translation of the *Homeric Hymn to Demeter*[62] and then weaved in various poems and prose by Crowley that related in some way to elements of the story. I hoped that when it was all put together and performed, it would evoke the appropriate mood. At least it would actually add a traditional *Eleusinian* rite to the *Rites of Eleusis*.

For several years we decorated our ancient garage as the underworld, and our groaning garage door opener served as the terrifying jaws of Hell, which yawned open to let Hades (me) snatch innocent Persephone (Constance) and carry her off to my underground kingdom—an act that thoroughly startled and delighted all in attendance.

The rite was great fun to present and became for us a permanent epilogue to our yearly rites season. In 1989, to observe the eleventh anniversary of the chartering of our lodge, I printed commemorative scripts of our Rite of Earth to give out as gifts to the cast, crew, and attending "mystes." These have become somewhat of a collector's item. It is now with the greatest pleasure that I present this rite to you. It represents, I believe, a fitting end to this little book of homemade magick. I hope you enjoy it.

The Rite of Earth
(from the Commemorative Handout)
Do what thou wilt shall be the whole of the Law.

Some of you might think it a bit presumptuous of me to add an eighth rite to Aleister Crowley's original seven Rites of Eleusis—and maybe you would be correct. Crowley's original series descends the Tree of Life from Binah (the sphere of Saturn) to Yesod (the sphere of Luna) but does not include a rite corresponding to Malkuth (the sphere of Earth). I certainly don't want people to think that the Rite of Earth is some recently unearthed Crowley manuscript or a lost *Liber*. It is not.

---

62. Adapted from the translation by Blaise Daniel Staples of the *Homeric Hymn to Demeter*, originally published in *The Road to Eleusis: Unveiling the Secret of the Mysteries* by R. Gordon Wasson, Albert Hofmann, and Carl A. P. Ruck. Thirtieth Anniversary Edition published by North Atlantic Books, copyright © 2008 by the R. Gordon Wasson Estate. Reprinted by permission of the publisher.

It is merely our attempt to capture and present a modest echo of the ancient Eleusinian Rite of Demeter. As no one knows exactly what the candidates (mystes) experienced at Eleusis, we can only speculate from the hints handed down through the works of Homer and a handful of others.

For our purposes, I have relied heavily on my savagely edited treatment of the *Homeric Hymn to Demeter*[63] as the narrative, coupled with selections from Aleister Crowley's epic poem *Orpheus*[64] and his visionary works *The Vision and the Voice*[65] and *Liber LXV,*[66] which I have used to move the play along. In addition to these selections, I've clipped the short prose piece "The Earth" from *The Equinox*, vol. I, no. 6[67] (which is the same volume that originally contained the seven Rites of Eleusis) and the poem "Nuit," also from *Orpheus*.

Crowley prefaced all his Rites of Eleusis with the astrologically appropriate section from J. F. C. Fuller's marvelous *Treasure House of Images*.[68] I have taken the liberty of doing the same with our little ritual.

Over the years, many people who have experienced the Rite of Earth tell us it is a fitting ceremony to conclude our seasonal performance of the Rites of Eleusis and have encouraged us to make it available. We are happy to be able to present it to you in this privately produced format. We hope you enjoy it.

---

63. Adapted from the translation by Blaise Daniel Staples of the *Homeric Hymn to Demeter*. Reprinted by permission of the publisher.

64. Aleister Crowley, *Orpheus, Liber Primus vel Carminum* (1907; Reprint, Chicago, IL: Yogi Publications, 1978).

65. Aleister Crowley, *The Vision and the Voice with Commentary and Other Papers*, "The Cry of the 9th Aethyr" (1922; Reprint, York Beach, ME: Weiser Books, 1998), pp. 174–175.

66. Aleister Crowley, *Liber LXV: Liber Cordis Cincti Serpente sub Figura* אדני—*The Holy Books of Thelema* (York Beach, ME: Weiser Books, 1983), p. 47.

67. Aleister Crowley, *The Equinox*, vol. 1, no. 6, edited by Soror Virakam (1911; Reprint, York Beach, ME: Weiser Books, 1992), pp. 108–111.

68. J. F. C. Fuller, *Liber DCCCCLXIII: The Treasure House of Images*, special supplement to *The Equinox*, vol. 1, no. 3 (1910; reprint, York Beach, ME: Weiser Books, 1992).

Konx Om Pax.
Love is the law, love under will.
Lon Milo DuQuette
Master, Heru-ra-ha Lodge O.T.O., January 7, 1989

The Rite of Earth
Dramatis Personae

HERMES. Messenger of the gods (in the guise of the poet Homer). Narrator and stage director. Yellow robe or toga. When acting as Hermes in the rite, he carries a caduceus.

DEMETER. Great earth-mother goddess. White robe or toga with green and gold accents. She is covered with a thick black cloak through part of the rite.

PERSEPHONE. Daughter of Demeter, wife of Hades. Diaphanous robe. When appearing as the wife of Hades, she is wrapped in a dark shawl and wears a golden crown.

HADES. God of death and the underworld. Black robe or toga. He wears a golden crown and holds a skull-topped scepter.

HECATE. Goddess of magic and protection. Black robe with hooded shawl. She holds a lamp or flame.

IRIS. Goddess of the rainbow and messenger of the gods. Rainbow robe with golden wings.

HERALD OF DARKNESS. Doorkeeper permitting exit from the citadel. Black robe from which hangs a large key. He or she holds a torch and an urn of wine.

HERALD OF LIGHT. Doorkeeper permitting entrance into the citadel. White robe from which hangs a large key. He or she holds an urn of wine.

OTHER GODS (if casting allows): POSEIDON, HELIUS, APOLLO, APHRODITE. These are minor officers in this particular ceremony. If there are not enough players, their lines may be spoken by Iris.

THE MYSTES. The audience participates throughout as the mystes— candidates for initiation into the Eleusinian mysteries.

Scenes

There are four scene locations (one indoors and three outdoors) that must be arranged so the officers and the audience en masse can move easily from scene to scene. They represent:

1. *The citadel of Eleusis.* The rite opens and closes in this indoor room. It should be large and open enough to comfortably accommodate the audience and cast. Ideally it should have a hearth or fireplace, comfortable chairs for those who need them, and an array of floor cushions for everyone else. In the opening scene, the citadel is dimly lit with a few candles; in the closing scene, it is brightly lit with many candles and lamps. Sweet-smelling incense is continually burning during both the opening and closing scenes.

The backyard of the venue should be large enough to accommodate three outdoor scenes, two at opposite corners of the yard (the garden of Persephone and the throne room of Hades) and a third directly in the center of the yard (the altar of Hecate).

2. *The garden of Persephone* is an open space in one corner of the yard planted with (or displaying pots containing) narcissus flowers.

3. *The throne room of Hades (the underworld)* is at the opposite corner of the yard and is an area enclosed by black hangings and strewn with skulls and bones and emblems of death. It should be illuminated to reveal the throne of Hades and the throne of his bride, Queen Persephone.

4. *The altar of Hecate* is located in the center of the yard. It is simply a waist-high altar or small table stand supporting a bowl of flaming

alcohol. There should be enough room around the altar for the mystes to circumambulate during Demeter's invocation of Hecate.

THE RITE OF EARTH

The rite begins in the dimly lit citadel of Eleusis, where the audience (the mystes) are comfortably seated or lounging on floor pillows. The atmosphere is relaxed. Candles and sweet-smelling incense are burning. For the moment, Persephone is the only cast member visible. When everything is ready, she stands and re-cites the "Twelvefold Renunciation of God and the Unity Thereof" from Liber DCCCCLXIII *(the Taurus chapter of the* Treasure House of Images*).*

PERSEPHONE:

The Chapter known as
The Twelvefold Renunciation of God
and the Unity thereof

I

adore

Thee by the

Twelve Renunciations

and by the Unity thereof.

1. O my God, Thou mighty One, Thou Creator of all things, I renounce unto Thee the kisses of my mistress, and the murmur of her mouth, and all the trembling of her firm young breast; so that I may be rolled a flame in Thy fiery embrace, and be consumed in the unutterable joy of Thine everlasting rapture.

2. O my God, Thou mighty One, Thou Creator of all things, I renounce unto Thee the soft-lipp'd joys of life, and the honey-sweets of this world, and all the subtilities of the flesh; so that I may be feasted on the fire of Thy passion, and be consumed in the unutterable joy of Thine everlasting rapture.

3. O my God, Thou Mighty One, Thou Creator of all things, I renounce unto Thee the ceaseless booming of the waves, and the fury of the storm, and all the turmoil of the wind-swept waters;

so that I may drink of the porphyrine foam of Thy lips, and be consumed in the unutterable joy of Thine everlasting rapture.

4. O my God, Thou Mighty One, Thou Creator of all things, I renounce unto Thee the whispers of the desert, and the moan of the simoom, and all the silence of the sea of dust; so that I may be lost in the atoms of Thy Glory, and be consumed in the unutterable joy of Thine everlasting rapture.

5. O my God, Thou Mighty One, Thou Creator of all things, I renounce unto Thee the green fields of the valleys, and the satyr roses of the hills, and the nymph lilies of the meer; so that I may wander through the gardens of Thy Splendour, and be consumed in the unutterable joy of Thine everlasting rapture.

6. O my God, Thou Mighty One, Thou Creator of all things, I renounce unto Thee the sorrow of my mother, and the threshold of my home, and all the labour of my father's hands; so that I may be led unto the Mansion of Thy Light, and be consumed in the unutterable joy of Thine everlasting rapture.

7. O my God, Thou Mighty One, Thou Creator of all things, I renounce unto Thee the yearning for Paradise, and the dark fear of Hell, and the feast of the corruption of the grave; so that as a child I may be led unto Thy Kingdom, and be consumed in the unutterable joy of Thine everlasting rapture.

8. O my God, Thou Mighty One, Thou Creator of all things, I renounce unto Thee the moonlit peaks of the mountains, and the arrow-shaped kiss of the firs, and all the travail of the winds; so that I may be lost on the summit of Thy Glory, and be consumed in the unutterable joy of Thine everlasting rapture.

9. O my God, Thou Mighty One, Thou Creator of all things, I renounce unto Thee the goatish ache of the years, and the cryptic books, and all the majesty of their enshrouded words; so that I may be entangled in Thy wordless Wisdom, and be consumed in the unutterable joy of Thine everlasting rapture.

10. O my God, Thou Mighty One, Thou Creator of all things, I
     renounce unto Thee the wine-cups of merriment, and the eyes
     of the wanton bearers, and all the lure of their soft limbs; so
     that I may be made drunk on the vine of Thy splendour, and be
     consumed in the unutterable joy of Thine everlasting rapture.

11. O my God, Thou Mighty One, Thou Creator of all things, I
     renounce unto Thee the hissing of mad waters, and the trum-
     peting of the thunder, and all Thy tongues of dancing flame;
     so that I may be swept up in the breath of Thy nostrils, and be
     consumed in the unutterable joy of Thine everlasting rapture.

12. O my God, Thou Mighty One, Thou Creator of all things, I
     renounce unto Thee the crimson lust of the chase, and the blast
     of the brazen war-horns, and all the gleaming of the spears; so
     that like an hart I may be brought to bay in Thine arms, and be
     consumed in the unutterable joy of Thine everlasting rapture.

13. O my God, Thou Mighty One, Thou Creator of all things, I
     renounce unto Thee all that Self which is myself, that black sun
     which shineth in Self's day, whose glory blindeth Thy Glory; so
     that I may become as a rushlight in Thine abode, and be con-
     sumed in the unutterable joy of Thine everlasting rapture.

O Glory be unto Thee through all Time
and through all Space: Glory,
Everlastingly. Amen,
and Amen, and
Amen.

Persephone exits the citadel.

The conductor, Hermes, enters and sits at the hearth. He encourages the mystes to make themselves comfortable and then relates to them the sacred story of Demeter and Persephone.

HERMES:

Let me sing to you the song of Demeter, holy Deo, the lady of the harvest, the great mother goddess whose hair grew in rich plaits, and of her daughter Persephone, whom Hades, the lord of the underworld, seized for his bride. Zeus, the thunder god, gave the girl to him as she was playing far from her mother gathering flowers with the daughters of the ocean. Earth brought forth the Narcissus to lure her. Amazed at the beauty of the flower, she stretched out both her hands to take it; as she did, the earth yawned open and Lord Hades burst forth from the underworld in a golden chariot drawn by his immortal horses. Screaming for pity and fighting him off, Persephone was dragged into the chariot, calling, "Father Zeus! Zeus!" But only the goddess Hecate, from her cave, and Lord Helius, the brilliant son of Hyperion, heard the poor girl's cries.

The peaks of the mountains echoed with her voice until at last her mother also heard her cries. So bitter was the pain that seized Demeter's heart that she tore the gossamer veil off her head and threw over her shoulders a great black cloak, the mantle of death.

Demeter flew swift as a bird over land and sea in search of her daughter, but no one, neither god nor mortal, dared tell her the truth. For nine days, holy Deo wandered the earth carrying blazing torches in her hands. So great was her grief that she refused the taste of ambrosia and the sweet nectar of the gods and shunned the bath. When dawn arrived on the tenth day, the goddess Hecate met her, holding a flame in her hand and bringing Demeter a message of her daughter's abduction—telling her of Lord Helius's knowledge of the details of the divine conspiracy between Zeus and Hades. Hecate and Demeter then sped straight to Helius, the sun, watchman of the gods and of men. Demeter said, "Helius, since we both are gods, you must help me! I bore a daughter, a beautiful child with a lovely face, whose cries I heard through uncharted skies, the cries of a captive—although I could not see anything with mine own eyes. But you, because you see everything, you must tell me the truth. Did you see what happened to my child?

Lord Helius replied, "Lady Demeter, you will know the truth. Zeus alone of the immortals is to blame, for he gave the child to Hades, his own brother, to have for his wife. But goddess, be comforted. Hades is your brother also, and is not an unfitting husband among the immortals. As for honor, he has his third of the world that he received when the realms were first apportioned. He is the lord over all those he received and all with whom he dwells."

Hearing this, Demeter's grief became anguish, and her heart swelled with wrath. Angry with Zeus, she shunned the assembly of gods on lofty Olympus and went in disguise to dwell among mortal men. No man or woman knew who she was. She arrived at length at the holy city of Eleusis, where the citadel sits like a crown upon the city—home of the honored and Celeus, who at the time was lord of Eleusis. Coaxed by the four daughters of Celeus, Demeter (looking like a crone) became the nurse of the newborn son of Celeus and Lady Mataneira.

During her stay with this blessed family the goddess refused all wine, taking only a mixture of barley and water, and the tender leaves of glechon. She would lift the little baby in her immortal hands and hold him to her fragrant breast to nurse him. The child flourished and grew like a god, for he fed not on mother's milk but on ambrosia with which Demeter anointed him—anointed as if born a god himself. She inspired him with her divine breath and sweetly rocked him in her lap. At night, in a secret ceremony, she would bury him in the powers of the fire upon the hearth to forge within him the magic of immortality. But his parents knew none of this, and to them the child seemed a miracle—a prodigy—somehow divine. Demeter would have made him ageless and immortal if not for the folly of Mataneira, his own mother.

One night, watching from the sweet-smelling chamber, she spied on the goddess at her magick and, alarmed by what she saw, shrieked in terror for her child. Enraged at this mortal interruption, Demeter grabbed the child from the fire and hurled him to the ground.

"All men are fools! They lack the sense to foresee their fate as it comes upon them—good or ill—whatever it may be. I swear by the river Styx, I would have made this child ageless for all time, and I would have granted him undying honor. Now he can never escape the demons that shall bring his death!"

As she said this, she transformed herself to her true and glorious beauty. The palace was filled with the terrible brilliance of a thousand bolts of lightning.

"I am Demeter, the one supreme in honor, for I am the source of life and joy both for mortals and immortals. This is what you must do: Have all your people build me a temple with an altar before it. Let it be built beside the fortress of the high city. I myself shall institute my rites so that you may perform them and, by doing so, appease my wrath."

When the people had finished the temple, they went home, each to his own house. But Demeter remained there, sitting apart from all the blessed gods and wasting away with longing for her daughter. Then she created a deadly year for mankind, withering the soil that once was so nourishing. The earth would not send up seeds because she kept them hidden.

Seeing this, Zeus feared in his heart that if mankind should perish, who then would honor and give sacrifice to the gods? So he sent Iris, who flies on wings of gold, to call upon Demeter and coax her back to the joys of Olympus. But Demeter's mind would not be changed. Then Father Zeus sent out all the blessed gods. One by one they went to her and gave her many splendid gifts and let her choose as much honor as she might want among the immortals. But none could persuade her to change her mind. She said she would never again set foot on Olympus or let the earth bear fruit unless she saw her daughter with her own eyes.

Finally Zeus sent Hermes to great Hades so that he might exhort him with soft words to let him lead holy Persephone out of the sunless west into the light. Then her mother would see her with her own eyes and change her mind.

So, leaving the seat of Olympus, Hermes obeyed and rushed through the hollows of the earth. He found the lord of the dead seated in his house on a couch with his awesome wife, but she was not there by her own will. She longed only to be with her mother, who was far away.

Hermes said to Hades, "Lord of death, Father Zeus commanded me to lead glorious Persephone out of Erebus and back to the gods to appease her mother's wrath and horrible anger against the gods. Demeter is planning a great act of vengeance. She is going to destroy the feeble race of mortals who dwell on earth and so cause the honors that are paid to the gods to perish."

Hades smiled and told Persephone that she could go and rejoin her mother and the gods. But first, he suggested she refresh herself by eating of a pomegranate. Secretly, he knew that if she ate of the fruit of the underworld, she could not remain forever with her mother, but instead must return to the underworld and spend one third of each year as his bride.

Hermes took Persephone to the temple of Demeter at Eleusis, where her mother awaited her. When she saw her daughter, Demeter ran to her like a maenad racing madly through mountain woods. Persephone, for her part, when seeing her mother's beautiful eyes, leaped from the chariot of Hermes and fell on her knees, embracing her mother.

The joyous reunion was marred by Demeter's discovery of Hades's trick, for she knew that if her daughter had taken food of the underworld, then their reunion must be broken for one third of each year. But their embrace finally softened their grief, each giving and receiving joy.

Then to them came Hecate, who wears a delicate veil. She also caressed the daughter of holy Demeter, and from that time on, Lady Hecate was the companion of Persephone. Father Zeus then sent Rhea, his own mother, to escort Demeter back to the race of the gods. Then Zeus promised to give her whatever honors she wanted from the immortal gods, and he consented to the plan that Persephone spend one third of each spiraling year in the dark, where the sun goes down, and two thirds with her mother and the other immortals. Then Demeter made fruits spring up from the rich plowlands and the whole world became heavy with leaves and flowers.

PART II

Hermes now marshals the mystes and prepares to lead them to the outdoor scene depicting the garden of Persephone. They are stopped at the door by the Herald of Darkness, who holds a torch and an urn of wine, which he empties onto the ground in front of them.

HERALD OF DARKNESS:
The voice of my Undying and Secret Soul said unto me, "Let me enter the Path of Darkness, and, peradventure, there I shall find the Light."

The Herald of Darkness then opens the door and lights the way for Hermes and the mystes. They enter the garden, where they find Persephone and the daughters of the ocean gathering flowers. Hermes narrates:

HERMES:
This is the daughter of the king. This is the virgin of eternity. This is she that the holy one hath wrested from the giant time, and the prize of them that have overcome space. This is she that is set upon the throne of understanding. Holy, holy, holy is her name, not to be spoken among men. For Kore they have called her, and Malkah, and Betulah, and Persephone. And the poets have feigned songs about her, and the prophets have spoken vain things and the young men have dreamed vain dreams; but this is she, that immaculate, the name of whose name may not be spoken. Thought cannot pierce the glory that defendeth her, for thought is smitten dead before her presence. Memory is blank and in the most ancient books of magick are neither words to conjure her, nor adorations to praise her. Will bends

like a reed in the tempests that sweep the borders of her kingdom and the imagination cannot figure so much as one petal of the lilies whereon she standeth in the lake of crystal, in the sea of glass.[69]

There was a maiden that strayed among the corn, and sighed; then grew a new birth, a narcissus, and therein she forgot her sighing and her loneliness. Even instantly rode Hades heavily upon her and ravished her away.[70]

The earth opens and Hades is seen abducting Persephone to his temple of the underworld.

PERSEPHONE:
Zeus! Zeus!

Following the abduction of Persephone, the temple of the underworld closes behind Hades and Persephone. Hermes directs the mystes to join him and follow Demeter on her journey in search of her missing daughter. In the process of her journey, they bear witness to her invocation of Hecate. (Demeter stands in the center of the yard, at the altar of Hecate. She lights the bowl of alcohol and recites the Invocation of Hecate. During the invocation, the mystes circumambulate Demeter and the flaming bowl nine times in a clockwise direction.)

DEMETER [Invoking HECATE]:[71]
O triple form of darkness! Sombre splendour!
    Thou moon unseen of men! Thou huntress dread!
    Thou crowned demon of the crownless dead!
O breasts of blood, too bitter and too tender!
    Unseen of gentle spring,

---

69. Aleister Crowley, *The Vision and the Voice with Commentary and Other Papers*, "The Cry of the 9th Aethyr" (1922; Reprint, York Beach, ME: Weiser Books, 1998), pp. 174–175.

70. Aleister Crowley, *Liber LXV: Liber Cordis Cincti Serpente sub Figura* אדני—*The Holy Books of Thelema* (York Beach, ME: Weiser Books, 1983), p. 47.

71. From Aleister Crowley's *Orpheus, Liber Primus vel Carminum* (1907; Reprint, Chicago, IL: Yogi Publications, 1978).

Let me the offering
　　Bring to thy shrine's sepulchral glittering!
I slay the swart beast! I bestow the bloom
Sown in the dusk, and gathered in the gloom
　　Under the waning moon,
　　　At midnight hardly lightening the East;
And the black lamb from the black ewe's dead womb
　　I bring, and stir the slow infernal tune
　　　Fit for thy chosen priest.

Here where the band of Ocean breaks the road
　　Black-trodden, deeply-stooping, to the abyss,
　　I shall salute thee with the nameless kiss
Pronounced toward the uttermost abode
　　Of thy supreme desire.
　　I shall illume the fire
　　Whence thy wild stryges shall obey the lyre,
　　Whence thy Lemurs shall gather and spring round,
Girdling me in the sad funereal ground
　　With faces turned back,
　　　My face averted! I shall consummate
The awful act of worship, O renowned
　　Fear upon earth, and fear in hell, and black
　　　Fear in the sky beyond Fate!

I hear the whining of thy wolves! I hear
　　The howling of the hounds about thy form,
　　Who comest in the terror of thy storm,
And night falls faster ere thine eyes appear
　　Glittering through the mist.
　　O face of woman unkissed
　　Save by the dead whose love is taken ere they wist!
Thee, thee I call! O dire one! O divine!
I, the sole mortal, seek thy deadly shrine,
　　Pour the dark stream of blood,

A sleepy and reluctant river
Even as thou drawest, with thine eyes on mine,
    To me across the sense-bewildering flood
        That holds my soul for ever!

    The night falls back;
        The shadows give place;
            The threefold form
    Appears in the black,
        As a direful face
            Half seen in the storm.
    I worship, I praise
    The wonderful ways
    Where the smitten rays
        Of darkness sunder.
    The hand is lifted;
    The gates are rifted;
        The sound is as thunder!
    She comes to the summons,
    Her face as a woman's,
        Her feet as a Fear's,
    Turned back on her path
    For a sign of wrath: —
        She appears, she appears!

At the conclusion of the invocation, the goddess Hecate appears before the altar of Hecate. She holds a lamp in her hands. She touches Demeter softly on the cheek, then points an accusatory finger toward the corner of the yard that conceals the throne of Hades. But before they travel there, they are met by Iris and the gods of Olympus.

IRIS:
    Ye fruits and corn,
        Gold, rose and green
    Vines purple-born,

Pearl-hidden sheen,
Trees waving in scorn
Of the grass between
Come forth in your chorus and chant raise of you mother and queen.
Most musical moves
The head of the corn;
Strong glorious loves
Of its being are born.
Dim shadows of groves
Of Demeter adorn
The waves and the woods of the Earth, the heart of the mother forlorn.

Turning to Demeter, Iris pleads:
Olympus alone
Of Earth's glories is taken
For Deity's throne
Deep-frozen, storm-shaken
What glories are shown
When their slumbers awaken!
The avalanche thunders adown, and the gods of the gods are forsaken.

POSEIDON (or other god or IRIS):
Wan grows Aphrodite
and Artemis frail;
Apollo less mighty.
Red Bacchus too pale.
Dark Hades grows bright.
He alone may avail
When the god and

Turning to Demeter, Poseidon pleads:
Olympus alone
Of Earth's glories is taken
For Deity's throne
Deep-frozen, storm-shaken
What glories are shown

When their slumbers awaken!
The avalanche thunders adown, and the gods of the gods are forsaken.

APOLLO (or other god or IRIS):
Ye trees many-fronded
   That shake to the wind,
  Green leaves that have sounded
   My harp in your kind,
  Light boughs that are rounded,
   Grey tops that are shrined
In the tears of the heaven as they fall, in the blackening storm grown blind!

  As mountains uplift
   As an arrow in air;
  Ice-crowned, rock-cliffed,
   Snow-Bosomed bare,
  I give you the gift
   Of a voice more fair,
Leave echo, and wake, and proclaim that ye stand against death and despair!

Turning to Demeter, Apollo pleads:
  Olympus alone
   Of Earth's glories is taken
  For Deity's throne
   Deep-frozen, storm-shaken
  What glories are shown
   When their slumbers awaken!
  The avalanche thunders adown, and the gods of the gods are forsaken.

The mystes are now led from the scene to the area outside the temple of the underworld. There they are met by Cerberus, who stands in the way. Hermes throws a honey cake to distract the three-headed dog. As Cerberus chases the honey cakes, Hermes is able to reveal the scene inside the temple of the underworld. All now can see Lord Hades seated on his throne with his lovely bride.

PERSEPHONE:

> Ah me! no fruit for guerdon,
> Who bore the blossom's burden.
> There shines no sunlight toward Persephone.
> Ravished, O iron-eyed!
> From my young sisters' side,
> Torn and dragged down below the sundered sea,
> No joy is mine in all thy bed,
> And all thy sorrow shaken on my head.

HADES:

Goddess, cease your great lament, for I am the brother of your father and mother and not an unfitting husband among the immortals. Zeus himself gave you to me for my bride. I am the lord of death and all things return to me. As for honor, you share with me the rulership of one third of the world.

PERSEPHONE:

Cursed above gods be thou
Whose blind unruffled brow
Rules the grim place of unsubstantial things!
Hated, to me thy face
Turns not the glance of grace.
I rule unloved above the infernal kings,
And only thee in all deep Hell
I charm in vain, despair my royal spell.
Thou mockest me with power;
Thy sceptre's awful dower
Avails me nothing...

Inexorable Lord!
Accursed and abhorred
Of men, begin in Hell to show thy grace!
Not to a man's weak life,
Not to thy shuddering wife,

But to the queen's unfathomable face
Dread beyond sorcery and prayer,
And fearful even because it is so fair!

Yea, from the ghastly throne
Unchallenged and unknown
Let the fierce accents roll athwart the skies!
My voice is given, my power
Fares forth to save the flower
Broken but plucked not by these fingers wise.
I love the song — be thou not mute,
But turn a lucky lot towards the suit!

HERMES (addressing HADES):
Lord of death, Father Zeus commanded me to lead glorious Persephone
out of Erebus and back to the gods to appease her mother's horrible anger against the immortals. Demeter has a furious wrath and won't min-
gle with the gods; instead, she sits apart from us in her fragrant temple,
which is scented with incense, and she holds as her domain now the rocky
citadel of Eleusis.

HADES:
This passes all. Relent. Release. Depart! I yield. My power is broken, and
my heart riven, and all my pride ruined, and me compelled to earth to
lose (Persephone).[72]

Hades offers Persephone the pomegranate. She eats three seeds.

---

72. Note: I altered this quote from *Orpheus: Liber Tertius vel Laboris*, which origi-
    nally read:
"This passes all. Relent. Release! Depart!
I yield: my power is broken, and my heart
Riven, and all my pride ruined, and me
Compelled to earth to loose Eurydice."

HADES:

Well be it so. O wizard, by this strength thou has availed in deepest Hell at length. I grant thy prayer. Persephone[73] is given to the sweet light and pleasant air of heaven! Even on this wise. With Hermes for a guide, up the dread steeps there followeth thee my bride.

PART III

Hermes and Persephone and the Herald of Darkness lead the mystes back to the (now brightly lit) citadel. They are barred at the threshold by the Herald of Light, who holds a torch and a full urn of wine. He empties the urn of wine on the ground and says:

HERALD OF LIGHT:

Light dawning in Darkness is thy Name,
Lord of the Universe … The vast and the Mighty One! Ruler of the Light and of the Darkness. We adore Thee and we invoke Thee!
Look with favour upon these Mystes and Grant thine aid unto the higher aspirations of their souls.

The Herald of Light stands aside and allows all to reenter the citadel, where they witness the reunion of Demeter and Persephone.

PERSEPHONE:

By the might of famine long
And supplication strong
Demeter won the swift Hermetic word!
In bitter days of eld
Thus by great force compelled

---

73. Note: I altered this quote from *Orpheus: Liber Tertius vel Laboris*, which originally read:
"Well, be it so. O wizard, by this strength
Thou hast availed in deepest Hell at length.
I grant thy prayer. Eurydice be given
To the sweet light and pleasant air of heaven!
Even on this wise. With Hermes for a guide
Up the dread steeps there followeth thee thy bride."

The glad Earth saw me, careless of my lord.
    Rise to her crystal streams and sapphire seas.

Mother and daughter embrace. Persephone continues:

Ah me! I feel a stirring in my blood
    Pours through my veins a delicate pale
      flood of memory, not the pale and
      terrible Goddess whose throne is manifest
      in Hell. I am again a child, a playful child.

INTERMISSION

The mystes applaud and find seats or floor pillows. The "gods" serve water and wine, dates, figs, dried fruit, and other delicacies. All enjoy a brief intermission and refreshments. Hermes and our actors stay in character and never allow the mystes to forget the ceremony is still in progress.

When the intermission is over and everyone is quiet again, Demeter stands and recites "The Earth."

DEMETER:

THE EARTH[74]

THE child of miracle to the world, greeting.

I reach my hands to the leaves and dabble in the dew: I sprinkle dew on you for kisses. I kneel down and hold the grass of the black earth to my bosom; I crush the earth to my lips as if it were a grape. And the wine of Demeter flushes my cheeks; they burn with joy of youth.

Why should I greet the world? Because my heart is bursting with love for the world. Love, say I? Why not lust? Is not lust strength, and merriment, and the famine that only the infinite can stay?

And why do I call myself the child of miracle? Because I have entered a second time into my mother's womb and am born. Because to

---

74. From Aleister Crowley's *The Equinox*, vol. 1, no. 6, edited by Soror Virakam (1911; Reprint, York Beach, ME: Weiser Books, 1992), pp. 108–111.

the knowledge of manhood has come the passion, even the folly, of ado-
lescence; with all its pride and purity.

It is for this that you see me lying upon the thick wet grass, unquench-
able; or rejoicing in the fat black loam.

Now the manner of the miracle was this. In the beginning is given
to a youth the vision of his mate. This one must he henceforth seek
blindly; and many are the enchantments and disenchantments. Through
this his vision fades; even his hunger dies away unless he be indeed Elect.
But in the end it may be that God shall send him the other half of that
Token of Paradise. Then, if he have kept the holy fire alight, perhaps
with much false fuel, that fire shall instant blaze and fill the temple of his
soul. By its insistent energy it shall destroy even the memory of all those
marsh-lights that came to greet it; and the priest shall bow down in the
glory, and grasp the altar with his hands, and strike it with his forehead
seven times. Now this altar is the earthen altar of Demeter.

Then understanding all things by the light of that love, he shall know
that this is love, that this is the soul of the earth, that this is fertility and
understanding, the secret of Demeter. Nay, (even!) the Oracle may speak
in his heart and foretell or foreshadow the greater mysteries of Persephone, of Death the daughter of Love.

Those, too, who are thus reborn will understand that I who write these
words am stretched on the wet earth on the day of Spring. It is night, but
only the sea whispers of Persephone, as the stars intimate Urania whose
mystery is the third, and beyond. My body is absorbed in scent and touch;
for the consuming fire of my sight has burnt itself out to blindness, and in
my mouth is only the savour of an infinite kiss. The moist earth burns my
lips; my fingers search down about the roots of the grass. The life of earth
itself is my life: I shall be glad to be buried in the earth. Let my body dissolve
into hers, putrefy in her reviving limbeck. He never loved who let them case
him in a coffin from the supreme embrace.

It is from the earth, bride of the sun, that all bodily strength derives. It
is no figure that Antaeus regained all his force when he touched earth. It is
no pedantry and folly of the Hindus, who (fearing bodily lust) isolate their
acolytes from earth, no futility their doctrine of Prana and the Tamo-Guna.
It is not mere faith healing, this hygiene of Father Kneipp, and his failures

are those who retain decorum and melancholy, who follow the letter and not the spirit, cold-blooded treaders upon earth instead of passionate lovers of its strength.

It is no accident of mythology that the Titans made war upon the Gods, and in Prometheus overthrew them.

It was when Canute failed to drive back the sea that his dynasty was lost to that Norman William who caught hold of Mother Earth with both hands.

When I was a child I fell; and the scars of the earth are on my forehead at this hour.

When I was a boy I was hurt by the explosion of a buried jar of gunpowder; and the scars of the earth are on my face at this hour.

Since then I have been the lover of the earth, that wooed me thus roughly. Many a night have I slept upon her naked breast, in forest and on glacier, upon great plains and upon lonely crags, in heat and cold, fair weather and foul; and my blood is the blood of the earth. My life is hers, and as she is a spark thrown off from the whirling brilliance of the sun, so do I know myself to be a spark of infinite God.

Seek earth, and heaven shall be added unto you! Back to our mother, drive the shining spade into her womb! Wrinkle her with your furrows, she will only smile more kindly!

Let your sweat, the sweat of your toil, which is your passion, drip like benediction from on High upon her; she will render corn and wine. Also your wife shall be desirable in your eyes all the days of your life, and your children shall be strong and comely, and the blessing of the Most High shall be upon you.

Then let your grasp relax in the satiety of death, and your weight shall cumber the earth, and the little children of the earth shall make merry with you until the rose strike its root into your breast. Then shall your body be one again with the mother, and your soul one with the Father, as it is written in the Book of the Law.

All this have I been taught by her whose purity and strength are even as Earth's, chosen before the foundation of Time. Lioness with lion, may we walk by night among the ruins of great cities, when, weary with happiness too great even for our immortality, we turn from the fragrance and fertility of Earth. And at the sunrise return where the peopled valleys call us; where, bronzed and buoyant, our children sing aloud as they drive home the spade.

Glory be to the Earth and to the Sun and to the holy body and soul of Man; and glory be to Love and to the Father of Love, the secret Unity of things!

Glory be to the Shrine within the Temple, and to the God within the Shrine, to the Word and to the Silence that bore it unto Him that is beyond the Silence and the Speech!

Also thanksgiving in the Highest for the Gift of all these things, and for the maiden in whom all these things are found, for the holy body and soul of man, and for the sun, and for the earth. AMEN.

Demeter sits among the mystes. Persephone stands and recites the "Exordium from Nuit."[75]

EXORDIUM FROM NUIT

Enough. It is ended, the story
   Of magical æons of song;
The sun is gone down in his glory
   To the Houses of Hate and of Wrong.
     Would ye see if he rise?
     In Hesperian skies
Ye may look for his rising for long.

The magical æon beginneth
   Of song in the heart of desire,
That smiteth and striveth and sinneth,
   But burns up the soul of the lyre:
     There is pain in the note:
     In the sorcerer's throat
Is a sword, and his brain is afire!

Long after (to men: but a moment
   To me in my mansion of rest)

---

75. From *Orpheus, Liber Quartus vel Mortis*, in *The Collected Works of Aleister Crowley*, vol. 3.

Is a sundawn to blaze what the glow meant
    Seen long after death in the west;
       A magical æon!
       Nor love-song nor pæan,
    But a flame with a silvery crest.

There shall rise a sweet song of the soul
    Far deeper than love or distress;
Beyond mortals and gods shall it roll;
    It shall find me, and crave, and caress.
       Ah! me it shall capture
       In torrents of rapture;
    It shall flood me, and fill, and possess.

For brighter from age unto age
    The weary old world shall renew
Its life at the lips of the sage,
    Its love at the lips of the dew.
       With kisses and tears
       The return of the years
    Is sure as the starlight is true.

Yet the drift of the stars is to beauty,
    To strength, and to infinite pleasure.
The toil and worship and duty
    Shall turn them to laughter and leisure.
       Were the world understood
       Ye would see it was good,
    A dance to a delicate measure.

Ye fools, interweaving in passion
    The lyrical light of the mind!
Go on in your drivelling fashion!
    Ye shall surely seek long and not find.
       From without ye may see

All the beauty of me,
   And my lips, that their kisses are kind.

For Eurodice once I lamented;
   For Orpheus I do not lament:
Her days were a span, and demented;
   His days are for aye, and content.
     Mere love is as nought
     To the love that is Thought,
   And idea is more than event.

O lovers! O poets! O masters
   Of me, ye may ravish my frown!
Aloof from my chocks and disasters!
   Impatient to kiss me, and crown!
     I am eager to yield.
     In the warrior field
   Ye shall fight me, and fasten me down.

O poets! O masters! O lovers!
   Sweet souls of the strength of the sun!
The couch of eternity covers
   Our loves, and our dreams are as done.
     Reality closes
     Our life into roses;
   We are infinite space: we are one.

There is one that hath sought me and found me
   In the heart of the sand and the snow:
He hath caught me, and held me, and bound me,
   In the lands where no flowers may grow.
     His voice is a spell,
     Hath enchanted me well!
   I am his, did I will it or no.

But I will it, I will it, I will it!
    His speck of a soul in its cars
Shall lift up immensity! fill it
    With light of his lyrical bars.
        His soul shall concentre
        All space; he shall enter
    The beautiful land of the stars.

He shall know me eternally wedded
    To the splendid and subtle of mind;
For the pious, the arrogant-headed,
    He shall know they nor seek me nor find.
        O afloat in me curled!
        Cry aloud to the world
    That I and my kisses are kind!

O lover! O poet! O maiden
    To me in my magical way!
Be thy songs with the wilderness laden!
    Thy lyre be adrift and astray:
        So to me thou shalt cling!
        So to me thou shalt sing
    Of the beautiful law of the day!

I forbid thee to weep or to worship;
    I forbid thee to sing or to write!
The Star-Goddess guideth us her ship;
    The sails belly out with the light.
        Beautiful head!
        We will sing on our bed
    Of the beautiful law of the Night!

We are lulled by the whirr of the stars;
    We are fanned by the whisper, the wind;
We are locked in unbreakable bars,

The love of the spirit and mind.
  The infinite powers
  Of rapture are ours;
We are one, and our kisses are kind.

HERMES:

Then Demeter went forth to the kings who administer justice: Triptolemus, and Diocles (who drives horses), and mighty Eumolpus, and Celeus (the leader of his people). To them she showed the performance of her rites and taught her mysteries—holy rites that are awesome, that no one may transgress, nor reveal, nor express in word, for an overwhelming reverence for the gods stops his voice.

Whoever among men walking the earth has seen these mysteries is blessed—but whoever is uninitiated and has not received his share of the rite, he will not have the same lot as the others—once he is dead and dwells in the mold where the sun goes down.

The entire casts of gods and heralds enter the citadel and array themselves around Demeter and Persephone.

HERMES (continues):

And when the goddess among goddesses had taught them everything, she went to Olympus to be in the company of the other gods. There the two goddesses live with Zeus, who delights in the thunderbolt, and they are holy and revered.

Whomever the goddesses love among men who walk the earth, he is blessed, for they soon send Plutus who gives wealth to mortal men.

Hermes now kneels before Demeter and Persephone.

HERMES (continues):

But come now, you goddesses who preside over the city of Eleusis, where incense perfumes the air—you two who also have domain on Paros, surrounded by the sea, and in mountainous Antron—you, Lady Deo, who brings in the seasons and gives splendid gifts; you and your beautiful daughter Persephone...come now, grant me an easy life for my song. And still again may I pray to sing you a song.

ENTIRE CAST AND MYSTES:
Konx Om Pax.

THE END

At the Gate of the New Year

Each year, instead of hosting a large, energy-draining New Year's Eve party that competes with a half dozen other large, energy-draining New Year's Eve parties thrown by our friends in neighboring Southern California communities, the DuQuettes host a different kind of event. We open our house to our partygoing friends who are traveling to or from bigger and wilder celebrations and give them a chance to pause and refresh themselves before going on to the great celebrations or returning home to their cozy beds. Our home is conveniently located midway on the party caravan trail between Los Angeles and South Orange County and San Diego, and a surprising number of vagabond revelers take advantage of our little way station.

Besides tea and snacks, we offer them the opportunity during their short visit to divine their fortunes for the coming year. If requested, I'll read their Tarot cards or help them with an *I Ching* or a geomantic reading. This quiet oasis during an otherwise loud and raucous day and night provides for many of our comrades a rare chance to truly reflect on their lives during the year that is passing away and the possibilities for the year to come—to look both forward and backward, like the two-faced Roman god Janus, god of gates and doors, beginnings and endings—and the month of January.

Our wayfarers' magical experience begins at the threshold of our front door. It's a simple ritual that was inspired by Constance's visit to the great temples of Japan. Before entering the temple, the pilgrims pause at an outdoor shrine and ceremonially wash their hands with pure water that is poured from a bamboo ladle. Then, with clean hands, they take a stick of incense and light it from a perpetual flame and place the burning incense in a container of sand. Sometimes they clap their hands as if to call the gods' attention to this offering, or else pause for meditation and prayer. Finally, they leave a few coins in another nearby vessel and continue their pilgrimage.

While our shrine is not as ornate as those of the Japanese temples, Constance nevertheless creates a beautiful version of this array of ritual objects on the stone bench that graces our tiny outer portico. There she places three large china bowls—one filled with pure water, one filled with sand, and one for coins. In the back of the bowl of sand, she places a lit votive candle. In front of everything, she stacks large amounts of Japanese stick incense.

And how do our guests know how to behave? Well, many of them know either from experience or from spiritual instinct what to do. But just in case, Constance posts a beautifully drawn and decorated sign that simply reads:

AT THE GATE OF THE NEW YEAR
New Year's Ritual of Welcome
Purify your hands with water so you may receive peace.
Light a stick of incense so you may receive freedom.
Offer a coin so you may receive stability.

Can you think of better gifts for the New Year?

KONX OM PAX

Eliphas Levi's "*Prayers to the Elementals*" [76]

PRAYER OF THE GNOMES OR EARTH SPIRITS

O Invisible King, who, taking the Earth for Foundation, didst hollow its depths to fill them with Thy Almighty Power. Thou whose Name shaketh the Arches of the World, Thou who causest the Seven Metals to flow in the veins of the rocks, King of the Seven Lights, Rewarder of the subterranean workers, lead us into the desirable Air and into the Realm of Splendour. We watch and we labour unceasingly, we seek and we hope, by the twelve stones of the Holy City, by the buried Talismans, by the Axis of the Lodestone which passes through the centre of the Earth—O Lord, O Lord, O Lord! Have pity upon those who suffer. Expand our hearts, unbind and upraise our minds, enlarge our natures.

---

76. From Eliphas Levi's *Dogme et Rituel de la Haute Magie* [Transcendental Magic: Its Doctrine and Ritual], 1854–1856. Translator unknown.

O Stability and Motion! O Darkness veiled in Brilliance! O Day clothed in Night! O Master who never doest withhold the wages of Thy workmen! O Silver Whiteness—O Golden Splendour! O Crown of Living and Harmonious Diamond! Thou who wearest the Heavens on Thy Finger like a ring of Sapphire! Thou who hidest beneath the Earth in the Kingdom of Gems, the marvelous Seed of the Stars! Live, reign, and be Thou the Eternal Dispenser of the Treasures whereof Thou hast made us the wardens. Amen.

PRAYER OF THE SYLPHS OR AIR SPIRITS

SPIRIT OF LIFE! Spirit of Wisdom! Whose breath giveth forth and withdraweth the form of all things:

THOU before whom the life of beings is but a shadow which changeth, and a vapour which passeth;

THOU who mountest upon the clouds, and who walkest upon the Wings of the Wind.

THOU who breathest forth Thy breath, and endless space is peopled;

THOU who drawest in Thy breath, and all that cometh from Thee returneth unto Thee!

CEASELESS MOTION in Eternal Stability, be Thou eternally blessed!

We praise Thee and we bless Thee in the Changeless Empire of Created Light, of Shades, of Reflections, and of Images, and we aspire without cessation unto Thy immutable and imperishable brilliance. Let the ray of Thy intelligence and the warmth of Thy love penetrate even unto us! Then that which is Volatile shall be Fixed; the Shadow shall be a Body; the Spirit of Air shall be a Soul; the Dream shall be a Thought. And no more shall we be swept away by the Tempest, but we shall hold the Bridles of the Winged Steeds of Dawn. And we shall direct the course of the Evening Breeze to fly before Thee! O Spirit of Spirits! O Eternal Soul of Souls! O imperishable Breath of Life! O creative sigh! O Mouth which breathest forth and withdrawest the life of all beings, in the flux and reflux of Thine Eternal Word, which is the Divine Ocean of Movement and of Truth! Amen.

Prayer of the Undines or Water Spirits

Terrible King of the Sea, Thou who holdest the Keys of the Cataracts of Heaven, and who enclosest the subterranean Waters in the cavernous hollows of Earth. King of the Deluge and of the Rains of Spring. Thou who openest the sources of the rivers and of the fountains; thou who commandest moisture which is, as it were, the Blood of the Earth, to become the sap of the plants. We adore Thee and we invoke Thee. Speak Thou unto us, Thy Mobile and changeful creatures, in the Great Tempests, and we shall tremble before Thee. Speak to us also in the murmur of the limpid Waters, and we shall desire Thy love.

O Vastness! wherein all the rivers of Being seek to lose themselves— which renew themselves ever in Thee! O Thou Ocean of Infinite Perfection! O Height which reflectest Thyself in the Depth! O Depth which exhalest into the Height! Lead us unto the true life through intelligence, through love! Lead us into immortality through sacrifice, that we may be found worthy to offer one day unto Thee, the Water, the Blood and the Tears, for the Remission of Sins! Amen.

Prayer of the Salamanders or Fire Spirits

Immortal, Eternal, Ineffable and Uncreated Father of all, borne upon the Chariot of Worlds which ever roll in ceaseless motion. Ruler over the Ethereal Vastness where the Throne of Thy Power is raised from the summit of which Thine Eyes behold all and Thy Pure and Holy Ears hear all—help us, thy children, whom Thou hast loved since the birth of the Ages of Time! Thy Majesty, Golden, Vast and Eternal, shineth above the Heaven of Stars. Above them art Thou exalted.

O Thou Flashing Fire, there Thou illuminatest all things with Thine Insupportable Glory, whence flow the Ceaseless Streams of Splendour which nourish Thine Infinite Spirit. This Infinite Spirit nourishest all and maketh that inexhaustible Treasure of Generation which ever encompasseth Thee replete with the numberless forms wherewith Thou hast filled it from the Beginning. From this Spirit arise those most holy Kings who are around Thy Throne, and who compose Thy Court.

O Universal Father, One and Alone! Father alike of Immortals and Mortals. Thou hast especially created Powers similar unto thy Thought Eternal and unto Thy Venerable Essence. Thou hast established them above the Angels who announce Thy Will to the world. Lastly, thou hast created us as a third Order in our Elemental Empire.

There our continual exercise is to praise and to adore Thy Desires; there we ceaselessly burn with Eternal Aspirations unto Thee, O Father! O Mother of Mothers! O Archetype Eternal of Maternity and Love! O Son, the Flower of all Sons! Form of all Forms! Soul, Spirit, Harmony, and Numeral of all things! Amen!

Index

A

A∴A∴, 5, 19, 27, 95

Abyss, 45, 48, 152, 169

aces, 111–114, 128

Ahathoor, 141

air (element), 38, 49, 55, 62, 63, 69, 71, 81, 98, 111, 112, 114, 115, 126, 129, 172, 175, 183, 189, 190

altar of Hecate, 159, 168, 170

AMORC (Rosicrucian Order), 5, 23, 25, 26

Aphrodite, 159, 171

Apollo, 159, 171, 172

Aquarius, 92, 114–116, 130, 152

archangel, 16, 39, 80, 98, 112

Aries, 112, 114, 116, 126, 129, 152

Assiah, 48

astrology, 92, 98, 125, 127

Atziluth, 48, 71

Interior Photo Credits

Page ix by Richard T. Wardell
Page 6 by Shirin Morton
Page 9 by Wayne Koehler
Page 17 by Richard T. Wardell
Page 86 by Richard T. Wardell
Page 87 by Jean-Paul DuQuette
Page 90 by Lon Milo DuQuette
Page 91 by Constance DuQuette
Page 92 by Lon Milo DuQuette
Page 97 courtesy of Lon Milo DuQuette
Page 105 by Lon Milo DuQuette
Page 121 by Lon Milo DuQuette
Page 122 by Richard T. Wardell
Page 138 by Richard T. Wardell
Page 150 by Richard T. Wardell
Pages 151–152 by Lon Milo DuQuette
Page 154 by Richard T. Wardell
Page 187 by Richard T. Wardell

To Write to the Author

If you wish to contact the author or would like more information about this book, please write to the author in care of Llewellyn Worldwide Ltd. and we will forward your request. Both the author and publisher appreciate hearing from you and learning of your enjoyment of this book and how it has helped you. Llewellyn Worldwide Ltd. cannot guarantee that every letter written to the author can be answered, but all will be forwarded. Please write to:

Lon Milo DuQuette
℅ Llewellyn Worldwide
2143 Wooddale Drive
Woodbury, MN 55125-2989

Please enclose a self-addressed stamped envelope for reply,
or $1.00 to cover costs. If outside the U.S.A., enclose
an international postal reply coupon.

Many of Llewellyn's authors have websites with additional information and resources. For more information, please visit our website at http://www.llewellyn.com.

LON MILO DUQUETTE

XARP
OMA
NTA
TOM

LOW MAGICK

IT'S ALL IN YOUR HEAD . . .
YOU JUST HAVE NO IDEA
HOW BIG YOUR HEAD IS

Low Magick
It's All In Your Head...

You Just Have No Idea How Big Your Head Is
LON MILO DUQUETTE

Take a fascinating journey into the life of one of the most respected, sought-after, and notorious magicians alive today: Lon Milo DuQuette. As entertaining as they are informative, the outrageous true stories in this one-of-a-kind memoir contain authentic magical theory and invaluable technical information.

DuQuette tells how a friend was cursed by a wellknown foreign filmmaker and how they removed that curse with a little help from Shakespeare. He explains how, as a six-year-old, he used the Law of Attraction to get a date with Linda Kaufman, the most beautiful girl in first grade. DuQuette also reveals the in and outs of working with demons and provides a compelling account of exorcising a demon from a private Catholic high school.

978-0-7387-1924-5, 216 pp., 6 x 9   **$16.95**

MODERN MAGICK

TWELVE LESSONS IN THE HIGH MAGICKAL ARTS

DONALD MICHAEL KRAIG

Modern Magick
Twelve Lessons in the High Magickal Arts
Donald Michael Kraig

For more than two decades, *Modern Magick* has been the world's most popular instruction manual on how to work real magick. Now, author Donald Michael Kraig, with decades more experience, research, training, and study, has created the ultimate version of this contemporary classic. This expanded edition features an updated design, more personal stories, and a wealth of new information, including more than 175 original images and a completely new chapter on three emerging trends in magick and how readers can put them to use. What hasn't changed: the comprehensive scope and clear, step-by-step ritual instructions that have made this book an indispensable guide for more than 150,000 magicians.

978-0-7387-1578-0, 528 pp., 8¹/₂ x 11   **$29.95**

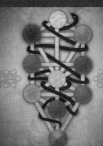

Magical Qabalah for Beginners
A Comprehensive Guide to Occult Knowledge
FRATER BARRABBAS

Qabalah comes from the Hebrew root QBL, which means "to receive or accept instruction." In *Magical Qabalah for Beginners,* Frater Barrabbas instructs the ritual magician and occult student on the history and theory of Qabalah as well as its practical ritual use. Using a combination of Greek philosophy and Jewish occultism, Frater Barrabbas presents the Qabalah in five basic but essential parts, covering the ten sephiroth, the twenty-two paths, the four worlds, the three negative veils, and the Tree of Life.

With practical tools and exercises, Frater Barrabbas shows how to make the Qabalah an important part of any occultist's spiritual and magical practice. Discover the essential tools for systematically incorporating the Qabalah into practical use: tables of correspondence, numerology, acronyms and formula, sigils and ciphers, contemplation, and the theurgy of ascension.

978-0-7387-3244-2, 360 pp., $5^{3}/_{16}$ x 8   **$15.99**

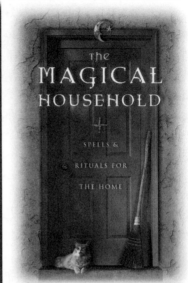

the
MAGICAL
HOUSEHOLD

SPELLS &
RITUALS FOR
THE HOME

SCOTT CUNNINGHAM & DAVID HARRINGTON

The Magical Household
Spells & Rituals for the Home
SCOTT CUNNINGHAM
DAVID HARRINGTON

Recognize and celebrate the magic of life with timeless rites and spells. Create a magical household—a haven of harmony, safety, spirituality, security, and romance. The benefits include a happier existence, protection against thieves, improved health, restful sleep, satisfying spiritual experiences, and a perfect environment for positive magic. This warm and wise guide by much loved author Scott Cunningham has been helping people create sacred space in their homes and gardens for nearly twenty years.

978-0-87542-124-7, 208 pp., 5¹/₄ x 8 $12.95

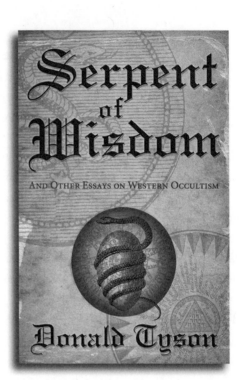

Serpent of Wisdom

of

AND OTHER ESSAYS ON WESTERN OCCULTISM

Donald Tyson

Serpent of Wisdom
And Other Essays on Western Occultism
DONALD TYSON

The sixteen essays in this collection deal with a wide variety of essential topics in Western occultism. They were written with the average reader in mind, so the material is not overwhelmingly technical. At the same time, very few writers have dealt with these subjects in the manner in which they are presented here: familiar topics with fresh insights that reconcile magic with rational thinking in a way that won't outrage the reason of intelligent readers. Subjects covered include energy, familiars, the magic circle, black magic, spirits' rights, the definition of magic, and much more.

978-0-7387-3618-1, 312 pp., 5³/₁₆ x 8   **$16.99**

The
ESSENTIAL
ENOCHIAN
GRIMOIRE

An Introduction to Angel Magick
from Dr. John Dee to the Golden Dawn

AARON LEITCH

The Essential Enochian Grimoire
An Introduction to Angel Magick from Dr. John Dee to the Golden Dawn
AARON LEITCH

Aaron Leitch, author of *The Angelical Language, Volume I*, and *The Angelical Language, Volume II*, has created the first how-to Enochian magick grimoire. This practical instruction manual outlines Enochian cosmology, the angels and the spirits of the system, the temple setup, and the making and usage of tools. It reveals the secrets and power of the classical Enochian system by Dee, as well as the modern version by the Golden Dawn, and provides rituals for each. All the angels' names are listed, along with exact instructions for summoning them and descriptions of how they should appear when summoned. Featuring almost 100 illustrations and tables for clarity, this is an important resource for both beginner and advanced practitioners alike.

978-0-7387-3700-3, 384 pp., 6 x 9   **$27.99**
